FOR ALL
GOD'S
WORTH

D0806905

Also by Tom Wright and published by SPCK

FOR ALL
GOD'S
WORTH

Tom Wright

TRIANGLE

First published in Great Britain 1997
Triangle
Society for Promoting Christian Knowledge
Holy Trinity Church
Marylebone Road
London NW1 4DU

British Library Cataloguing-in-Publication Data
A catalogue record of this book is available from the British Library

ISBN 0-281-05045-7

Printed in Great Britain by
Biddles Ltd, Guildford and King's Lynn

for the musicians of Lichfield Cathedral

Contents

INTRODUCTION

How can you cope with the end of a world and the beginning of another one? How can you put an earthquake into a test-tube, or the sea into a bottle? How can you live with the terrifying thought that the hurricane has become human, that fire has become flesh, that life itself came to life and walked in our midst? Christianity either means that, or it means nothing. It is either the most devastating disclosure of the deepest reality in the world, or it's a sham, a nonsense, a bit of deceitful play-acting. Most of us, unable to cope with saying either of those things, condemn ourselves to live in the shallow world in between. We may not be content there, but we don't know how to escape.

This little book is an attempt to say that the way through is by sheer unadulterated worship of the living and true God, and by following this God wherever he leads, whether or not it is the way our traditions would suggest. Worship is not an optional extra for the Christian, a self-indulgent religious activity. It is the basic Christian stance, and indeed (so Christians claim) the truly human stance. 'Worship' derives from 'worth-ship': it means giving God all he's worth. Hence the title of this book.

For many, Christianity is just a beautiful dream. It's a world in which everyday reality goes a bit blurred. It's nostalgic, cosy, and comforting. But real Christianity isn't like that at all. Take Christmas, for instance: a season of nostalgia, of carols and candles and firelight and happy children. But that misses the point completely. Christmas is not a reminder that the world is really quite a nice old place. It reminds us that the world is a shockingly bad old place, where wickedness flourishes unchecked, where children are murdered, where civilized countries make a lot of money by selling weapons to uncivilized ones so they can blow each other apart. Christmas is God lighting a candle; and you don't light a candle in a room that's already full of sunlight. You light a candle in a room that's so murky that the candle, when lit, reveals just how bad things really are. The light shines in the darkness, says St John, and the darkness has not overcome it.

Christmas, then, is not a dream, a moment of escapism. Christmas is the reality, which shows up the rest of 'reality'. And for Christmas, here, read Christianity. Either Jesus is the Lord of the world, and all reality makes sense in his light, or he is dangerously irrelevant to the problems and possibilities of today's world. There is no middle ground. Either Jesus was, and is, the Word of God, or he, and the stories Christians tell about him, are lies.

This is the conviction that has shaped this book. If the word 'god' refers to anything, and if that anything is anything like the God revealed in Jesus of Nazareth, then we are bound to take this God with the utmost seriousness. (There are, of course, all sorts of historical and theological problems involved in making claims like this about Jesus and God; I am doing my best to address them elsewhere.) We can't just acknowledge a God like this at a distance, and carry on as before. If the stories are true, this God didn't stay at a distance himself. He took us seriously enough to come into our world as one of us.

But if we take this God seriously, we find we have to take ourselves seriously as well. Not, of course, in the sense that we become gloomy or morbid; rather, in the sense that we must look at ourselves in the mirror and ask some fairly sharp questions about who we are and what we think we're up to. If God is God, these questions are worth asking. If Jesus is the Word of God, the answers might just take your breath away – and offer you God's breath instead. When that happens, the first result is worship, worshipping God for all he's worth; and the next result will be mission. That movement, that rhythm, is what this book is all about.

Most of this book has grown out of that rhythm as it is expressed in the life and work of Lichfield Cathedral, which, like all cathedrals, is designed to house a community of worship and mission. The second chapter is based on the sermon which I preached at my installation as Dean; several other chapters began in the cathedral as well. The early chapters focus quite narrowly on God and on what worshipping God actually means. The later ones address a range of issues in the mission and unity of the church which arise from that worship. A cathedral, after all, is not a place of retreat from the world, but a place of prayer and of prophecy, a beacon to shine God's light into the world. It is designed as a rich and powerful symbol of the gospel of God's grace.

One of the supreme ways in which a cathedral can be this in reality is by using God's gift of music both in worship and in witness. Hence the dedication: to a group of people whose particular vocation is to enable the rest of us, in the cathedral and further afield, to lift our hearts and minds to the living God in worship and adoration, and to respond to him in love and service. Church musicians sometimes come in for a bad press – from the clergy, for being obstinate and intractable (which of course clergy *never* are themselves!); from the public, either for being out of touch or for being impossibly trendy. I am delighted to report that none of these things apply to our present musicians, from the Organist and Master of the Choristers, Andrew Lumsden, down to the youngest chorister. On the contrary, they exemplify the Lichfield Cathedral motto, *Inservi Deo et Laetari*: Serve God and be cheerful!

Taking daily and weekly worship seriously needs serious resources. All the proceeds from this book will go towards the maintenance and enhancement of the musical life of the cathedral, as we seek to serve the local community, the whole diocese of Lichfield, and the wider church and world. It is my hope that the book will thus, in a small way, help to enable the thing which it commends.

Tom Wright
Lichfield Cathedral

Part One: The God Who is Worthy of Praise

CHAPTER ONE

Worship

What is the most beautiful thing you have experienced this week?

Maybe something you heard. Maybe some beautiful music – perhaps in church, or in a cathedral.

Maybe something you saw in the world of nature: the sun breaking through the mist and making the autumn leaves luminous; the curl of a squirrel's tail as he sat nibbling a nut.

It might be something you smelt: the scent of a rose, perhaps, or the smell of a good meal cooking when you were very hungry.

It might be something you tasted: an exquisite wine, a special cheese, that same meal well seasoned and well cooked.

Maybe something you experienced in work: things suddenly coming together, an unexpected new opportunity.

It might be something you experienced in human relationships: a quiet, gentle glance from someone you love dearly; the soft squeeze of a child's hand.

Hold the moment in your mind. And ask yourself: what does this beauty do to you?

It enriches you; yes. It warms you inside; yes. It makes you more alive; yes. It makes you stronger; yes. It makes you, perhaps, a little humble: you didn't cause this beauty, you didn't make it, it just happened, and happened to you. Yes.

And what does this beauty call out from you?

Gratitude – of course; delight – yes, naturally; a sense of awe – well, perhaps; a sense of longing for something beyond, something just out of reach – quite possibly, though if your experience of beauty was the smell of a good meal I hope it didn't stay out of reach for too long.

What about – *worship*?

Does beauty call out worship from you?

We don't very often use the word 'worship' to describe our attitude to things or people other than God himself. Almost the only place we come across it is in the marriage service in the Book of Common Prayer, where, to my mind utterly appropriately, the man declares to the woman, 'with my body I thee worship'. And, of course, there are good biblical injunctions not to worship, in the fullest sense, anything or anyone except God himself. But the word 'worship' means, literally, 'worth-ship': to accord worth, true value, to something, to recognize and respect it for the true worth it has. And that sets us on a trail that leads us from the squirrel in the garden, the steak in the oven, the singing in the choir, and the squeeze of the hand, all the way to the one who created all of them in the first place.

I want to speak about worship; and that means that I want to talk about God, and about the beauty of God. If we are to worship God truly, it is not enough to think of God's greatness and majesty, his power and sovereignty, his holiness and absolute otherness. That's all enormously important, as part of the story. But we wouldn't ordinarily use the word *beauty* to refer to any of that. I want to suggest to you in this chapter that our ordinary experiences of beauty are given to us to provide a clue, a starting-point, a signpost, from which we move on to recognize, to glimpse, to be overwhelmed by, to adore, and so to worship, not just the majesty, but the beauty of God himself. And, just as we don't very often use the word 'worship' in connection with beauty in the natural world, so we don't very often use the word 'beauty' in connection with God. That is our loss, and I suggest we set about making it good.

Why do I want to talk about worship? Two reasons stand out. First, there are some central passages in scripture which speak of our citizenship in heaven, and which speak of it not least as a constant and delighted experience of worship. The great multitude in Revelation which no man can number aren't playing cricket. They aren't going shopping. They are *worshipping*. Sounds boring? If so, it shows how impoverished our idea of worship has become. At the centre of that worship stands a passage like Isaiah 33: your eyes will see the king in his beauty; the LORD is our judge, the LORD is our ruler, the LORD is our king; he will save us. Worship is the central characteristic of the heavenly life; and that worship is focused on the God we know in and as Jesus.

The second reason I want to talk about worship is that it forms the central task of the church, not least of a cathedral. The Archbishops of Canterbury and York recently commissioned a report on English cathedrals, which was published in 1994 under the title *Heritage and Renewal* (London: Church House Publishing). The report covers many different aspects of the life of Cathedrals. Whatever one thinks of the details in various places, there is, right at the centre, something they got gloriously right. The report states unequivocally and emphatically that the purpose of a cathedral – and this would, of course, apply to any church anywhere – is worship and mission. These two, it emphasizes, belong inextricably together, with management (which it calls 'governance') as the vital means of enabling and sustaining that worship and mission. 'There is unanimity', they say, 'about the priority of worship in the function of cathedrals . . . These great buildings are descriptions of the majesty of God; places of living faith' (p. 8). The Commission stresses that, at the centre of all mission opportunities and management requirements, the primary emphasis is on worship as 'the maintenance of a daily witness to the sovereignty of God in the world' (p. 15). This is linked directly to the cathedral's role in society, and always has a missionary reference: 'in giving glory to God, the primary purpose of worship, those present may be enabled to catch a glimpse of that glory' (p. 17). Daily cathedral worship has been 'the central pillar of the Church's prayer and praise down the centuries, and the spiritual heartbeat not only of the cathedral but of the diocese, the community and the nation' (p. 18). Indeed, it is the worship of God that prevents these buildings becoming mere theme parks or museums: 'Without the warming fire of worship', say the Commission in summing up at the end of the report, 'these elegant buildings would be ancient monuments rather than living temples capable of inspiring the souls of men and women with glimpses of the divine' (p. 173).

It is right, therefore, that from time to time the church should take stock of that which is most central, most important, most vital in our common life together. Though we sing with the tongues of men and of angels, if we are not truly worshipping the living God, we are noisy gongs and clanging cymbals. Though we organize the liturgy most beautifully, if it does not enable us to worship the living God, we are mere ballet-dancers. Though we repave the floor and reface the stonework, though we balance our budgets and attract all the tourists, if we are not worshipping God, we are nothing.

Worship is humble and glad; worship forgets itself in remembering God; worship celebrates the truth as God's truth, not its own. True worship doesn't put on a show or make a fuss; true worship isn't forced, isn't half-hearted, doesn't keep looking at its watch, doesn't worry what the person in the next pew may be doing. True worship is open to God, adoring God, waiting for God, trusting God even in the dark.

Worship will never end; whether there be buildings, they will crumble; whether there be committees, they will fall asleep; whether there be budgets, they will add up to nothing. For we build for the present age, we discuss for the present age, and we pay for the present age; but when the age to come is here, the present age will be done away. For now we see the beauty of God through a glass, darkly, but then face to face; now we appreciate only part, but then we shall affirm and appreciate God, even as the living God has affirmed and appreciated us. So now our tasks are worship, mission and management, these three; but the greatest of these is worship.

And do you see why it's so easy to create that pastiche of 1 Corinthians 13, substituting 'worship' for 'love'? Worship is nothing more nor less than love on its knees before the beloved; just as mission is love on its feet to serve the beloved – and just as the Eucharist, as the climax of worship, is love embracing the beloved and so being strengthened for service.

But this is only true if it's the true God you're worshipping. I was talking to somebody not long ago who said, 'You know, I used to believe in God; but then, as I grew up, I found it harder and harder to think of this old man up there in the sky, so far removed from all the pain and suffering down here in the world.' And I said to him, 'I don't

believe in that god either! The God I believe in is the God I
see in the middle of the pain and the suffering down here in
the world. Without Jesus, the crucified Jesus, sharing and
bearing the pain and sin and suffering of the world, I don't
actually know who on earth, or in heaven, God might be at
all.' You see, if you envisage a god up there in the sky,
detached from the reality of the world, any worship you
offer will simply be a distant acknowledgement of majesty,
like the ploughboy doffing his cap as the great nobleman
rides by ignoring him. And if you go the other route, as my
friend was inclined to, and say that therefore the word
'god' can only refer to the impulse of goodness inside ourselves, then you'll find it pretty hard to sustain any real
sense of worship at all. All you're left with is the ploughboy imagining himself to be a nobleman. But if Jesus is to
be the lens through which you glimpse the beauty of God,
you will discover what it means to worship, because you
will discover what it means to be loved.

Put it this way: if your idea of God, if your idea of the
salvation offered in Christ, is vague or remote, your idea of
worship will be fuzzy and ill-formed. The closer you get to
the truth, the clearer becomes the beauty, and the more you
will find worship welling up within you. That's why theology and worship belong together. The one isn't just a head-
trip; the other isn't just emotion.

I recently read a remarkable testimony to this fact, from
a man called Jason Richards, who at the time was in Park-
hurst prison serving a life sentence for murder. This is
some of what he said:

I hadn't been long in my sentence and I was very con-
fused . . . I was carrying an awful lot of guilt. I was
looking for answers. I read a lot. I read Buddhism. I
read Islam. I started reading the Bible. And the more I
read the Scriptures the more I became aware of God.

I didn't believe in God. I was actually an atheist – or at least I thought I was. But I came to believe that God existed. And the more I became aware of God the more I became aware that I was a sinner – and I got more and more desperate.

Then one night . . . I opened the Bible at the very first psalm. I started reading . . . and when I got to Psalms 50 and 51 I realized that God would forgive me. I didn't know [why Psalm 51 had been written] then. But the thing I knew was, 'Save me from bloodguilt, O God, the God who saves me, and my tongue will sing of your righteousness.'

I knew that God could forgive me . . . I didn't know anything about Jesus or the Bible or the Church. I just knew. I read all the rest of the psalms on my knees – and almost from that point for me they became psalms of praise. *It was like I was beginning to worship – and I didn't know what worship was.*

From one point of view that last sentence is no doubt true. He didn't know the dictionary definition of worship. He probably didn't even use the word itself. But I think he did know what worship was, because I think he had met the living God, the loving God, the beautiful God, the God of whom the psalmist wrote when he said:

> One thing have I desired of the LORD, that I will require:
> That I may dwell in the house of the LORD all the days of my life,
> To behold the fair beauty of the LORD, and to visit his Temple.

The beauty of God is the beauty of love; love in creation, love in re-creation of a world spoiled by sin. It is the same love; which is why all the beauty of the world, the beauty that calls forth our admiration, our gratitude, our worth-ship at the earthly level, is meant as a set of hints, of conspiratorial whispers, of clues and suggestions and flickers of light, all nudging us into believing that behind the beautiful world is not random chance but the loving God. He who made the eye, does he not see? He who made the ear, does he not hear? He who created all beauty, is he not himself beautiful? Woe betide those who offer to the creature the worship due to the creator alone; but woe betide those who fail to read the hints, who fail to hear the subtext, who have the experience but miss the meaning, who are deaf to what may be heard, half-heard, in the stillness between two waves of the sea.

St Augustine, in a famous passage, rightly denies that our loves for the material world are the same thing as love for God. Yet, he says, our loves for the material world give us both a sign of, and the vocabulary for, our love for God. And we don't have to apologize for speaking of this love in this way. The world is God's creation, and its beauty is the steady, quizzical pointer to the beauty of God. This is what he wrote:

> What do I love when I love my God? Not physical beauty, or the splendour of time; not the radiance of earthly light, so pleasant to our eyes; not the sweet melodies of harmony and song; not the fragrant smell of flowers, perfumes, and spices; not manna or honey; not limbs such as the flesh delights to embrace. These are not the things that I love when I love my God.
>
> And yet, when I love him, I do indeed love a certain kind of light, a voice, a fragrance, a food, an embrace; but this love takes place in my inner person, where my soul is bathed in light that is not bound by space; when it listens to sound that time never takes away; when it

breathes in a fragrance which no breeze carries away; when it tastes food which no eating can diminish; when it clings to an embrace which is not broken when desire is fulfilled. This is what I love when I love my God. *(Confessions* 10.6)

People often quote Oscar Wilde's dictum, that a cynic knows the price of everything and the value of nothing. We live in an age of cynics, where 'worth' means 'price' and 'price' means money and money means power. But the gospel of Jesus Christ puts worth back into the world, worth beyond price, worth beyond worldly power; for the gospel of Jesus Christ summons us to worship, to worthship, to lay our lives before the one true and living God, to worship him for all he's worth. Give to this great and loving God the honour, the worship, the love, due to him; celebrate the goodness, the worth, the true value, of the created order, as his gift, his handiwork; and allow that celebration to lift your eyes once more to God himself, to his glory and beauty.

This is, of course, precisely what we do in the Eucharist. Symbols of the natural world become vehicles of the heavenly world, of which we are called to be citizens. And it is utterly fitting that we should surround and celebrate this moment of intense beauty with carved stone and coloured glass, with soaring music and solemn ritual. Worship is what we were made for. Worship is what buildings like churches and cathedrals were made for. If we get this right, we will go to our tasks of mission and management in the right spirit and for the right reason. Worship the LORD in the beauty of holiness; let the whole earth stand in awe of him.

CHAPTER TWO

It Is All God's Work

It is all too easy to suppose that, when we turn from worship to work, we turn from thinking about God to thinking about ourselves. Not so, says St Paul in a magnificent passage in 2 Corinthians 5.11-21: 'It is all God's work' (v. 18). It isn't just us playing ceremonial games; it isn't us forcing our agendas on to people; it isn't a few religious nuts coming unscrewed and rattling around the place. What we are about is the work of God.

Now of course that's an absurd claim. Surely God does God's work; who are we to claim to have even a small hand in it? Well, which god might we talking about? A god who is so lofty and remote that he would never get his hands dirty? That's not the God that great cathedrals were designed to celebrate. A god who is identified with the processes of nature? That's not the God whom the early missionaries went all over the world to proclaim. No: the God we worship here is the God of costly love: 'The love of Christ', Paul wrote, 'overwhelms us, when we consider that one died for all; and his purpose in dying was that those who live should live no more for themselves, but for him who for their sake died and was raised.' In other words, there is a different God to those imagined by so many in the dark ages both of the seventh century, when the first Christian communities were founded in Middle England, and of the late twentieth century. The true God is the one who became human and died and rose again in order to offer a new way of being human, a way of worship and love. Christ died, says Paul, so that we might embody the saving faithfulness of God: 'It is all God's work.'

Now if that isn't true, a building like a cathedral is simply an expensive monument to an impossible dream; and all we do in it is simply an elaborate way of turning over in bed, the better to continue the dream rather than wake up and face reality. But if it is true – if it really is the case that the true God is the one whose love overwhelms us in Jesus Christ – then the appropriate response is celebration, because this God is the reconciler, the healer. Celebration and healing: that is what a cathedral is all about.

'It is all God's work'; celebration no less than anything else. We in the modern West have forgotten *how* to celebrate, probably because we've forgotten *why*. Large meals, lots of drink, and behaving childishly is a parody of true celebration; but it's what you might expect when we forget that our maker is also our lover. That was the condition of Israel in exile, the people addressed in Isaiah 35. Israel was called to be the people of God, but in exile it had all gone stale. People in our society know in their bones that they are made to reflect God's image; but they feel exiled, futile, and stale; so they go in for tired and shoddy celebration, seen only too clearly in the forced frivolity of television programmes over Christmas and New Year. Contrast that mood with the one Isaiah held out to the exiles:

The wilderness and the dry land shall be glad,
  the desert shall rejoice and blossom;
like the crocus it shall blossom abundantly,
  and rejoice with joy and singing . . .
They shall see the glory of the LORD,
  the majesty of our God.

> . . . the ransomed of the LORD shall return,
>   and come to Zion with singing;
> everlasting joy shall be upon their heads;
>   they shall obtain joy and gladness,
>   and sorrow and sighing shall flee away.

When we realize once again that our God is the one who loves us into new life, then we will really know how to celebrate. True celebration, in turn, sustains true humanness. As we glimpse the living God, we are transformed into his likeness.

So it isn't surprising that those who are grasped by this gospel have built cathedrals. People who have forgotten who God is produce concrete jungles and cardboard cities. People who remember or rediscover who God is build cathedrals to his glory, and homes where the poor are cared for; we have both in the city of Lichfield, and they belong together, in celebration and healing. People in our contemporary society are cramped and stifled, fed on a diet of ugliness and noise. They are hungry for beauty, for light, for music. In celebrating and maintaining a wonderful cathedral, we are not a sub-branch of the 'heritage industry'. We are telling real people about the real God: we are saying that there is a different way to be human, a way in which worship and mystery and silence and light and space all play their proper part.

Thus, in a generation whose daily diet is the trivia of muzak and the relentless cacophony of industrial noise, we have the opportunity to celebrate the love of God with some of the greatest music ever written. In doing so, we are not a sub-branch of the musicians' union, but are creating the conditions for real people to be caught up in a rhythm of worship which is beyond their own power, and which can often refresh the parts other styles cannot reach. 'It is all God's work': beauty springs out of naught at the touch of

God. That is why we celebrate; and every gift that God has given us, of art, architecture, music, flower-arranging, theological study, and everything else, is taken up within the total sacrifice of praise. That's what a cathedral is there for. It is all God's work.

But celebration is only the beginning; and in some ways it isn't the most important part of the story. The first time I was shown around Lichfield Cathedral the thing that struck me most forcibly was the way in which the building itself had suffered over the years. The scars are still there; the seams still show, and the stitching is still visible, where devastation in one generation met with reconstruction in the next. Lichfield suffered more than any other cathedral during the Civil War; it was used variously as a military stronghold and as a stable, and it lost its central tower in the process. And there are older tales, too, of massacres and violence. Treasures have been plundered, not least the relics of Chad himself, the first Bishop. Looking wider than just the building, the diocese of Lichfield has suffered various identity crises, being redefined as much because of political intrigue as because of spiritual or pastoral necessity. So, too, the history of both the chapter and the choir reveals all too clearly the folly, as well as the faith, of our forebears. It is even reported that there have been some Deans who were less than the perfect model of Christian piety and wisdom; though one suspects, of course, that here at least malicious legend has been at work.

So what? Is all this something over which we should draw a discreet veil? Should we quietly forget the past, and just enjoy our building and music? No; that would turn the place into a compromise between a museum and a concert hall. Rather, we should embrace the fact that the very stones of such a building speak of a God who takes human wrath and turns it to his praise; who takes even Christian folly and turns it into wisdom; who takes wickedness done in his own name and brings out of it restoration, reconciliation, and new life. If the gospel of Jesus Christ is not about God doing precisely that, it is no good to us. This building embodies the word we need to hear, the word that Isaiah announced to the exiles:

> Then shall the eyes of the blind be opened
> and the ears of the deaf unstopped;
> then shall the lame leap like a hart,
> and the tongue of the dumb sing for joy;
> for waters shall break forth in the wilderness,
> and streams in the desert.

Yes, it is a scandal that Lichfield Cathedral should have functioned as a convenient spot from which to shoot people. Yes, it is somewhat ambiguous that it was restored under Charles II. Yes, it is to our shame that the history of our church is littered with disputes and squabbles. But let's get hold of one thing: St Chad did not come to Lichfield to tell people that if they were already good enough God would be happy to have them on his side. The eighth-century Lichfield Gospels, which we treasure in the cathedral, were not lovingly illuminated because they said that if the people of God were without blemish then God would bring in his kingdom. No. The reason why Chad came to Lichfield, and the reason why an ancient scribe lavished such craftsmanship on those priceless pages, is quite simply that the message *in* those Gospels is even more priceless: the message, that is, that the true God takes our brokenness and in Christ makes us new; that he picks up the pieces of our life, yes, even of our muddled attempts to follow him, and sticks them together again in a new way; that he heals those who are broken in heart, and gives the medicine to heal their sickness; that he promises new life, resurrection life, beyond all our sickness and death. To celebrate precisely here is to celebrate not the wonderful achievements of the church but the healing power of God to build his church with battered and broken building-blocks, including people like you and me. Celebration and healing; it is all God's work.

And what if the seams are still visible? What if the stitching still shows? What if we carry about with us the pain of being half put back together and half still in pieces? What if we have identity crises, if we live with ambiguities and face problems we can't solve overnight? Is that not what being a Christian is all about? As Paul continues, we are taken for imposters, and yet are genuine; dying, and behold we live; in pain, yet always full of joy; poor, yet making many rich; having nothing, yet possessing everything. Paul is not describing an occasional unfortunate lapse from the norm. This is normal Christian existence.

It is because people forget this that much nonsense is spoken and written today. From time to time in the UK certain journalists enjoy mocking the Church of England for having lost its nerve. We are hopelessly divided, they say, heading for ruin, going round in circles like a rudderless ship, with our leaders in disarray and our people in confusion. The evidence they cite consists, often enough, of quotations from each other, and from a suspiciously short list of would-be spokesmen (they're usually men) from the church.

I wonder which world these people live in? Where is it written in scripture that we can expect the church to be free from financial problems, from doctrinal controversy, from difficulties about leadership, from deep personal and corporate anxieties? Where is it written in history that there ever was such a church? Where is it written in theology that God demands such perfection? Go back to Paul's second letter to Corinth and you will find that it concerns exactly these issues. And Paul addresses his readers in Corinth, not with carping criticism, but with the power of love; not with sneering put-downs about what a shabby lot they were in Corinth, but with the gospel of Jesus; not with cynicism, but with the cross.

And the cross – as the very shape of the cathedral, like so many churches, reminds us – the cross is the be-all and end-all of the gospel. It is the cross that generates celebration and offers healing. It is all God's work: the cross speaks of the God who didn't send someone else to do the dirty work but came and did it himself; of the God who lived in our midst and died our death; of the God who now entrusts us with that same vocation. Because of the cross, being a Christian, or being a church, does not mean claiming that *we've* got it all together. It means claiming that *God's* got it all together; and that we are merely, as Paul says, those who are overwhelmed by his love. A cathedral is not the triumphalistic sign of a careless power and prestige; it is the covenant sign of a suffering love, the symphony in stone in honour of the Servant King.

And if the seams are still visible – if the stitching still shows – so what? Those journalists of whom I spoke should leave their comfortable metropolis for a moment and come here; come and worship with us, share our life for a few days; then come round the diocese and see the new green shoots that are growing through the secular concrete; look where the blind are seeing, and the lame walking, and the dumb singing for joy. Let them come and see where the diocese, whose mother church this is, is standing alongside those recently unemployed in the mining areas; let them see that the countryside may be forgotten by the politicians but is not forgotten by the church; let them see how priests ordained right here are working with the people of the street in Walsall and Wolverhampton. Let them come and see that we, gladly together with all who name the name of Jesus, are following as best we know how in the way of the cross. Of course we are in pain on various issues. Of course we sometimes feel as if we're coming unglued. So what? Let them come and see that at the heart of England there is a building whose very stones speak of God's healing love; that at the heart of that building there is a book whose every page is a work of art celebrating that love; and that around that book there is a community of people committed to the one of whom that book speaks, who know themselves called to live not for their own sakes but for his sake who died and rose again. This is our God, the Servant King; he calls us now to follow him.

And if we are to make such an invitation, our immediate task is to consolidate what this community is already good at. No one comes into this cathedral, or into any church, without some pain or fear, without some guilt or grief. But the testimony of many is that when they have come here they have felt welcomed, loved and sustained. That is wonderful, and I thank God for it. People have learned elsewhere today to expect rudeness and even violence as the norm. They are thirsty for gentleness, for kindness, for the sense that they matter. They need to be shown that there is a different way of being human, that the true God embraces them, as they are, with the healing power of the cross and the life-giving breath of the Spirit. That welcome is our work, because it is all God's work, and he invites us to share in it.

We are therefore, in Paul's words, to be ambassadors for Christ. We don't have to be perfect in ourselves. On the cross he dealt with our sin so that he could then work through us, so that we in turn might embody the saving faithfulness of God to all those whom we meet, all those who enter here. And the real mystery of that is that we do it not so much in our triumphs as in our tragedies; not in our strength but in our weakness; not in our success but in our failure. In the real world, it is the wounded who heal.

That is why the chequered history of this cathedral forms such an eloquent statement of the gospel. Celebration and healing: this is to be a place where eyes are opened to truth, where ears long deaf hear their name spoken in love, where those who had forgotten how to sing discover a joy which refuses to remain silent. And when *we* live by that gospel, then tourists may find themselves becoming pilgrims; photographers may stop clicking for a moment and glimpse true beauty; musicians may hear undreamed of harmonies; and historians may come face to face with the one who is Lord of the dead and the living. And so, as celebration leads to healing, healing leads back to celebration. It is all God's work; and those who find themselves called to it must, quite simply, 'serve God and be cheerful'.

CHAPTER THREE

The God I Want?

A few years ago I was browsing in a second-hand bookshop when I came across a book with a title that still makes me think. I confess I didn't buy the book, and haven't read it, so I don't know if I am misjudging it and its author; but the title sums up a particular attitude shared by many people, including many Christians, today. The title was *The God I Want*. I remember thinking then, and I still think now, that that title was silly, and ultimately self-defeating.

The God I Want? Left to myself, the god I want is a god who will give me what I want. He – or more likely it – will be a projection of my desires. At the grosser level, this will lead me to one of the more obvious pagan gods or goddesses, who offer their devotees money, or sex, or power (as Marx, Freud and Nietzsche pointed out). All idols started out life as the god somebody wanted.

At the more sophisticated level, the god I want will be a god who lives up to my intellectual expectations: a god of whom I can approve rationally, judiciously, after due consideration and weighing up of theological probabilities. I want this god because he, or it, will underwrite my intellectual arrogance. He will boost my sense of being a refined modern thinker. The net result is that *I* become god; and this god I've made becomes my puppet. Nobody falls down on their face before the god they wanted. Nobody trembles at the word of a home-made god. Nobody goes out with fire in their belly to heal the sick, to clothe the naked, to teach the ignorant, to feed the hungry, because of the god they wanted. They are more likely to stay at home with their feet up.

But on one particular day in the year we celebrate the God whom we didn't want – how could we have ever dreamed of it? – but who, amazingly, wanted us. In the church's year, Trinity Sunday is the day when we stand back from the extraordinary sequence of events that we've been celebrating for the previous five months – Advent, Christmas, Epiphany, Lent, Good Friday, Easter, Ascension, Pentecost – and when we rub the sleep from our eyes and discover what the word 'god' might actually mean. These events function as a sequence of well-aimed hammer-blows which knock at the clay jars of the gods we want, the gods who reinforce our own pride or prejudice, until they fall away and reveal instead a very different god, a dangerous god, a subversive god, a god who comes to us like a blind beggar with wounds in his hands, a god who comes to us in wind and fire, in bread and wine, in flesh and blood: a god who says to us, 'You did not choose me; I chose you.'

You see, the doctrine of the Trinity, properly understood, is as much a way of saying 'we don't know' as of saying 'we do know'. To say that the true God is Three and One is to recognize that if there is a God then of course we shouldn't expect him to fit neatly into our little categories. If he did, he wouldn't be God at all, merely a god, a god we might perhaps have wanted. The Trinity is not something that the clever theologian comes up with as a result of hours spent in the theological laboratory, after which he or she can return to announce that they've got God worked out now, the analysis is complete, and here is God neatly laid out on a slab. The only time they laid God out on a slab he rose again three days afterwards. On the contrary: the doctrine of the Trinity is, if you like, a signpost pointing ahead into the dark, saying: 'Trust me; follow me; my love will keep you safe.' Or, perhaps better, the doctrine of the Trinity is a signpost pointing into a light which gets brighter and brighter until we are dazzled and blinded, but which says: 'Come, and I will make you children of light.' The doctrine of the Trinity affirms the rightness, the propriety, of speaking intelligently about the true God, while at the same time affirming intelligently that the true God must always transcend our grasp of him, even our most intelligent grasp of him. As St Paul says, what matters isn't so much our knowledge of God as God's knowledge of us; not, as it were, the god we want but the God who wants us. God help us, we don't understand ourselves; how can we expect to understand that Self which stands beside our selves like Niagara beside a trickling tap?

All of this leaves me with two questions. First, do we then need to say anything at all? Isn't it enough just to acknowledge that the whole thing is extremely mysterious and puzzling and leave it at that? Mightn't we just as well say that god is five and one, or fifteen and one, as that God is Three and One? Second, and most important, what difference does it make in what we please to call 'the real world'?

These two questions are in fact intimately linked. We can make 'intelligent' missiles that can make war on one particular building hundreds of miles away, but we don't have an equivalent one that can make peace. Might that be because we have worshipped the gods of war, but have forgotten about worshipping the prince of peace? We can put a few men on the moon, but the few men who were standing between the Tutsis and the Hutus in Rwanda in 1994 had to be withdrawn for lack of funds and political will. Might that be because we have worshipped the gods of technology, the gods who boost our own national security –

the gods we have wanted, in other words – and have forgotten the god who asked Cain, 'Where is Abel your brother?'

You see, what you believe about God makes a difference to the way you respond to this god, and at the same time to the way you are in the world. Let's look at the options. For most people in the Western world today, the word 'god' refers to a distant, remote being. We can't and don't know very much about this being. He may or may not have made the world, though if we say he did we have an uncomfortable feeling that the scientists are going to challenge us (despite people like John Polkinghorne in Cambridge, one of the finest scientists of our generation and also a leading Christian theologian). This god may or may not intervene from time to time in the world, though he usually doesn't. He has, in fact, left us to muddle through as best we can; which usually means looking after our own interests, carving up the world, and perhaps each other, in our own way. The cat's asleep upstairs, and the mice – and perhaps the rats – are organising the world downstairs.

That's why this remote 'god' is the god that the Western world decided it wanted in the eighteenth century: a god to be cooly acknowledged for an hour or so on Sunday mornings, and ignored for the other hundred and sixty-seven hours in the week. No wonder, when they did a survey not long ago, the great majority of people in the United Kingdom said they believed in 'god', but only a small minority regularly go to church. If that's what you believe about 'god' – and it's what a lot of our society still does believe, including (alas) some within the church – then any sense of worship or religious celebration becomes a vague ritual, a meaningless noise, which merely makes us feel a bit better about ourselves. Is it any wonder that the rats are eating the dead after yet another massacre, and the dove is still locked up in the ark? Can such a god really be God?

The problem is that when you banish what you call 'god' up into the remote stratosphere, other gods come clamouring for attention from closer at hand. There are very few out-and-out atheists in the world; those who claim to disbelieve often merely disbelieve in the old high-and-dry god, while happily serving other gods of whom they may be quite unaware, and doing so not just for one hour in the week but with total energy and commitment. I have spoken of the gods of war, of money, of sex. The appalling genocide that still continues in our contemporary world, even within supposedly 'civilized' parts of it, are evidence that millions still give allegiance to gods of blood and soil, of tribe and race. Sometimes they try to invoke parts of Christian tradition to support this; but the fact that they go on killing each other shows clearly enough that it isn't Jesus whom they are worshipping. Christian doctrine isn't a matter of intellectual algebra. It is directly integrated with the way people behave. If the gods you want, and worship, are the gods from below, the local tribal gods, the gods of power and wealth and pleasure, you will destroy yourself and everyone who gets in the way.

But what if we were to take the doctrine of the Trinity seriously? What sort of response, what sort of worship, would that generate? And what sort of agenda, what sort of programme, might arise from such worship?

Before we can address this question, we must face the problem: why on earth should we think in trinitarian terms at all? Isn't this just a bit of muddled dogma, a jumble of dusty ideas which may have meant something to someone many years ago, but about which we must keep a newly open mind today?

The short response to that was given some time ago by G. K. Chesterton. The purpose of an open mind, he said, is like the purpose of an open mouth: that it might be shut again on something solid. Yes, we must be free to ask questions. But when we hear a good answer we must be prepared to recognize it as such, and not be so keen on keeping all questions open that we shy away from an answer because we so like having an open mind. That is the way to intellectual, as well as spiritual, starvation.

But the fuller answer might run something like this. I set it out in three brief stages: it would, of course, take an entire course in systematic theology to work it out in detail.

First, the place of doctrine within Christianity is absolutely vital. Christians are not defined by skin colour, by gender, by geographical location, or even, shockingly, by their good behaviour. Nor are they defined by the particular type of religious feelings they may have. They are defined in terms of *the god they worship*. That's why we say the Creed at the heart of our regular liturgies: we are defined as the people who believe in this god. All other definitions of the church are open to distortion. We need theology, we need doctrine, because if we don't have it something else will come in to take its place. And any other defining marks of the church will move us in the direction of idolatry.

Second, despite what is often imagined, the Trinity grows directly out of Jewish monotheism. It isn't a later corrupt development. The Jewish belief in one god, which was the seed-bed for early Christianity, was never intended as an analysis of the inner being of this one god. Rather, within Judaism in the time of Jesus we find various ideas about the way the one god would act within his world. He would come to live in the Temple. He was present when people studied his law. He breathed with his Spirit on certain persons, to enable them to speak and act with his authority. He spoke his creative Word, and things happened. His divine Wisdom was alive and active throughout the world, but especially in Israel. And it is precisely these ideas – these thoroughly Jewish ways of envisaging the one true and living God – that form the basis of what the earliest Christians said about Jesus and the Spirit. They didn't imagine for a moment that they were abandoning Jewish-style monotheism. They simply used the Jewish categories available to them to describe what it was that they had seen in Jesus, and what it was that they knew of the Spirit. The doctrine of the Trinity is thoroughly present in the very earliest writings of the New Testament, such as Paul's letters: God was in Christ reconciling the world to himself, and entrusting us (by the Spirit) with the message of reconciliation. Trinitarian theology is not a late or strange corruption. It lies at the heart of the very earliest Christianity of which we have evidence.

Third, the particular words we use to express trinitarian theology are of course negotiable. The word 'person', for instance, doesn't mean in modern English what it meant in the Latin from which the phrase 'three persons' is derived. This is the point at which we must be truly open-minded. The doctrine of the Trinity, indeed, is paradoxically the thing which forces us to keep our minds open: having grasped, or been grasped by, the fact that the true god is both three and one we are forced not into closed-mindedness but into true open-mindedness, not because we want to criticize or dispute but because we are hungry for God, hungry to know him better, hungry to love in return the one, and the three, who has loved us into life. The word 'person' in speaking of the Trinity is a way of saying that, from one point of view, there is an irreducible three-ness about the true God, and that the man Jesus of Nazareth is to be identified with one of these three. Likewise, the word 'substance', in speaking of the Trinity, is a way of saying that, from another point of view, there is an irreducible oneness about the true God, shared completely by Jesus and by the Spirit. If we can find better ways of saying the same thing, good luck to us.

I return, then, to my underlying question. What sort of response might belief in this God generate? What sort of spirituality does such worship foster? What sort of agenda might it generate?

To believe in the Trinity is to believe that the true god is the passionate and compassionate God. He is neither the high-and-dry, remote god of so much modern imagination, nor the dark force that drives people into selfish and destructive lifestyles. He is the God who gives himself totally to his world, gives himself in sacrificial love, pours himself out generously, recklessly and prodigally upon his creation. When St John the Divine found himself looking into the open door of heaven, he didn't see the god he might have wanted; he saw all creation worshipping the awesome and majestic creator God; and, when he looked closer, he saw a Lamb that had been killed and was now alive for evermore. The doctrine of the Trinity declares the mystery which is above all else what this broken world needs to hear: that the true God is not detached from the evil of the world, but has come to share it and bear it in his own body. We do not say, 'God so loved the world that he sent somebody else'; we say, 'God so loved the world that he sent his only beloved Son.'

And, as St Paul insists, the God who sent the Son is the God who sends the Spirit of the Son, to put into practice, to implement, what the Son achieved. To believe in the Trinity is to believe that God came in Jesus to the place where the pain was greatest, to take it upon himself. It is also to believe that God comes today, in the Spirit, to the place where the pain is still at its height, to share the groaning of his world in order to bring the world to new life. But the Spirit doesn't do that in isolation. The Spirit does it by dwelling within Christians and enabling them to stand, in prayer and in suffering, at that place of pain. The doctrine of the Trinity is all about prayer, and pain, and prophecy.

It is the doctrine that undergirds the work of a Mother Theresa. It is the doctrine that assures us that our visiting of the sick, our teaching of the young, our creating of beauty, our praying and working for justice and peace in the world, are not simply us doing something for God; they are God acting in and through us.

Moreover, the doctrine of the Trinity assures us that this work is not in vain. Even if, like Jesus himself, we seem to have thrown ourselves away chasing a dream that many dismiss as foolish or impossible, the doctrine of the Trinity insists that out of this death there comes new life, God's own life given to be the life of the world. As we pray for those places in the world which undergo intense and utterly horrible suffering, we stand with those Christians who are at the place of pain right now, continuing through their tears to bear witness to the suffering love of the true God; and we pray for strength to say prophetically to our own government, and to other people's governments, and to the United Nations, that there is a different way of ordering international affairs, and that we must seek and find it with all urgency.

And so it is not as an escape from the world, but as the only truly human stance before the world, that we affirm our faith in the one God who is Father, Son and Spirit. And we do that not just in words, in saying the Creed. We do it, far more powerfully, in the symbol of the Eucharist. The Eucharist is all about God's life given in Jesus Christ to be our life. It is all about God's Spirit, the Spirit of Jesus, given now to be our breath of life. As we eat and drink, we become walking shrines, living temples, in whom the living triune God truly dwells. And if this scary thought should make us take our fellow Christians more seriously as what they really are, it should also make us take more seriously the tasks to which the living God calls us within his world. We cannot worship the suffering God today and ignore him tomorrow. We cannot eat and drink the body and blood of the passionate and compassionate God today, and then refuse to live passionately and compassionately tomorrow. If we say or sing, as we so often do, 'Glory be to the Father, and to the Son, and to the Holy Spirit', we thereby commit ourselves, in love, to the work of making his love known to the world that still stands so sorely in need of it. This is not the god the world wants. This is the God the world needs.

CHAPTER FOUR

God on the Same Scale

When my family and I lived in Montreal, one of our constant sources of amusement was the inability of British visitors to grasp the sheer scale of North America. The province of Quebec alone is the size of Western Europe. To get from Montreal to Vancouver you have a longer journey than to get from London to Montreal in the first place. What we had to do from time to time was to get one of those maps of Canada which have a tiny little map at the side, labelled 'Britain on the same scale'.

Now supposing you had something that worked the other way round. Supposing you had an ordinary map of Britain in an atlas, and then, on the facing page, you had a folded-up insert, which was labelled 'America on the same scale.' You would spread it out on a table, fold after fold after fold, until it filled half the room, completely dwarfing the ordinary map of Britain. No one who had seen that would ever again make the mistake of thinking, as some of our visitors did, that they could pop over to San Francisco in the car for a day visit.

That is the effect that the author of Isaiah 40 intends to create. The people he is addressing have scaled down their god to fit their own stunted imagination. So he starts with their world – the world of geography, of politics, of religion, of astronomy – and he proceeds to sketch, as it were, God on the same scale. There it is, fold upon fold upon fold, laid out before us:

> Who has measured the waters in the hollow of his hand, weighed the mountains in scales and the hills in a balance?
> The nations are like a drop in a bucket, like dust on the scales;
>> idols are made of wood, plated with gold and silver;
>> earth's inhabitants are like grasshoppers before him;
>> he brings princes to naught, and makes the rulers of the world as nothing;
>> he created the stars, bringing them out and counting them, calling them by name, checking that they are all present.

Get your mind round that, says Isaiah; or rather, open your mind wider, so that it can take it in. You can't measure God on the map even of the world's greatest features. Nor is God simply bigger than them, as though God were a Deist god, simply the most important being in a sequence of beings. You need a different sort of scale altogether, a different set of dimensions.

And why does Isaiah write this stunning piece of poetry? Not as a piece of speculative theology. Not simply in order to rebuke the small-mindedness of his contemporaries' theology. He writes in order to lift up the hopes, as well as the eyes, of a broken and disillusioned people: 'Comfort, comfort my people, says your God; speak tenderly to Jerusalem, and cry to her that her warfare is finished, her penalty paid; she has received from YHWH's hand double for all her sins.' The greatness of this God does not detach him from his people; it means, on the contrary, that he is close enough to comfort them, gentle enough to be their shepherd, strong enough to give them strength:

He will feed his flock like a shepherd, and gather the lambs in his arm, and gently lead the mother sheep;

he gives power to the faint, and strengthens the powerless.

Even youths will faint and be weary, and young people fall exhausted;

but those who wait for YHWH shall renew their strength, they shall mount up with wings like eagles; they shall run and not be weary, they shall walk and not faint.

The chapter begins with the message of comfort, which continues by describing the prophetic voice which will ring out:

In the wilderness prepare the way of YHWH; make straight in the desert a highway for our God . . .

The glory of YHWH shall be revealed, and all flesh shall see it together; for the mouth of YHWH has spoken.

The people are in Babylon; but their hearts and spirits are in the wilderness, in no man's land, in the country where they think nobody loves them, everybody's forgotten them, and they have no hope of anything ever being any different. Listen to it again:

Why do you say, O Jacob, and speak, O Israel, 'My way is hidden from YHWH, and my right is disregarded by my god'?

And in this wilderness, their God, the powerful one, the creator of the ends of the earth, will come to them again, will come and meet them, come like a shepherd looking after his lambs, gently leading the mother sheep. He will reveal his glory, and all flesh shall see it together. This is the good news that the herald must tell:

> Get up to a high mountain, you herald of good tidings to Zion;
> lift up your voice with strength, you herald of good tidings to Jerusalem.
> Lift it up, do not fear; say to the cities of Judah: 'Look! Here is your God!'

The prophet is quite explicit. The people of Israel have got so used to the map of their own present experience – their tragedy, their hopelessness, their forgottenness, their exile – that they have imagined that their god is somehow contained on the same map. They have *tamed* their god; they have him like a pet, on the end of a lead, and he can't do them any good. And the prophet unfolds before them this huge, sprawling map of the untameable God – the creator, the Lord of the world, the gentle shepherd, the returning king – and says: Now, here is the one you can lean on. Here is the one you can trust. He has dealt with your sin, your failure, your tragedy. From now on he will reveal his glory, and he will reveal it in saving you and shepherding you. And Isaiah goes on to explain how God will do this, in terms of the strange servant-figure, the one who carries YHWH's saving purposes in his own self into the wilderness, into the exile, to the point of death and out the other side.

Let me bring this message twenty-five centuries forward, to our own day. One of those held hostage in Lebanon from 1985 to 1990 was the Irish writer Brian Keenan. In his awesome book *An Evil Cradling* (London: Vintage, 1993) he describes how, in solitary confinement, he and John McCarthy had, to their own surprise, been confronted with a reality that they had to call God, even though this reality was far bigger than his upbringing in nominal Christianity had taught him to expect. Listen to what he says, and think what an indictment this is (God help us) of much would-be Christian talk about God:

> At times God had seemed so real and so intimately close. We [Keenan and McCarthy] talked not of a God in the Christian tradition but some force more primitive, more immediate and more vital, a presence rather than a set of beliefs . . . In its own way our isolation had expanded the heart, not to reach out to a detached God but to find and become part of whatever 'God' might be . . . On occasion there would be discussions on vaguely religious themes, but they were certainly not confined by the dictates of strait-laced doctrines. We had each gone through an experience that gave us the foundations of an insight into what a humanized God might be. (p. 99)

Notice how Keenan equates the Christian tradition with a set of beliefs, and with 'strait-laced' doctrines. One wonders if he had ever heard Isaiah 40 read out in church, or heard a sermon preached on it. The 'god' of his upbringing seems to have been the Deist god: remote, detached, to be described in arid intellectual propositions, not the wild, untameable God of Isaiah, the creator, the Lord of the ends of the earth, who is also the gentle shepherd, the strong one who enables the crushed, the lonely, and the weak to lean on him and find new strength.

One could go further. What Keenan discovered, as he squatted in his solitary cell, coming to terms with his own wilderness, was – irony of ironies – the beginning of the fact of the Trinity, the fact which precedes and underlies all the doctrines. Listen to it again: 'We had each gone through an experience that gave us the foundations of an insight into *what a humanized God might be*.' One might almost think that he had been reading St Mark.

Mark's first fourteen verses appear quite artless: a simple description of John the Baptist and his baptism of Jesus, terse to the point of being almost laconic. He begins with two Old Testament quotations, both about the God who comes to his people at last, after their exile, after the death of their hopes and possibilities. The second of these, which he flags up for us, is by now familiar:

The voice of one crying in the wilderness,
Prepare the way of the Lord,
Make his paths straight.

He applies this, of course, to John the Baptist, coming in the wilderness with his baptism of repentance. And commentators have queued up to say: Silly old Mark, picking a cheap proof-text out of the hat! Just because John was 'in the wilderness', Mark thinks that somehow John is fulfilling Isaiah's prophecy.

But Mark knows exactly what he's doing. Isaiah was talking about the time when, at long last, the exile of God's people would come to an end, when God would comfort them, would feed his flock like a shepherd, would reveal his glory so that all the world might see. Had that happened, between Isaiah's day and the coming of John the Baptist? Virtually all Jews of the time would answer, of course not. They had come back from Babylon, but the great promises hadn't come true yet. They were still ruled over by one pagan nation after another, and YHWH had not returned to live with his people and save them. Isaiah prophesied about how the exile would end: a herald would cry out to Jerusalem and all Judaea that sins were now being forgiven – in other words, that the exile was coming to its end; and that Israel's god himself, YHWH, would come and save her. Mark tells of how John called the people of Jerusalem and all Judaea to his baptism for the forgiveness of sins; and of how he spoke of one coming after, who was stronger than he was, who would complete what he had begun. Anyone reading Mark with Isaiah in mind knows what to expect. We expect YHWH himself, Israel's god, the strong one, the creator of heaven and earth, the gentle shepherd, the coming king.

With breathtaking simplicity, Mark turns our eyes to look at this great sight: and we see – Jesus. In case we fail to get the point, Mark tells us that, at Jesus' own baptism, the voice from heaven addressed him in words echoing, among other passages, the great opening servant-song in Isaiah: you are my child, my beloved one, with you I am well pleased. Like Isaiah's servant (42.1), this strange king is anointed with YHWH's own spirit, to be his person for his task.

This, you might think, is revolutionary enough. But then this king, this YHWH-in-person, this stronger than strong one who submits to Israel's baptism of repentance, is himself driven out by the Spirit into the wilderness, to be tested within an inch of his life by the enemy, the accuser. He goes into the wilderness, because that is where his way has been prepared. He then comes back to Galilee, announcing the good news that Israel's god is at last becoming king. We find ourselves back with Brian Keenan, alone in his private wilderness, discovering a presence more primitive, 'more immediate and more vital', than 'a set of beliefs'. We are back in the prison cell, the place where one is tested to the limit, and, it seems, beyond. We are at the place where one discovers, not some strait-laced doctrine, but 'the foundations of an insight into what a humanized God might be'.

What effect does all this have on our thinking, our praying, and our living in the late twentieth century? There has recently been a small renaissance in trinitarian theology. We were confidently told by some theologians in the 1960s that the Trinity was out-of-date nonsense; but the doctrine is now being rediscovered as a source of power and illumination. But God forgive us if we ever forget that the doctrine is simply a shorthand for the story, and that the central character in the story is more primitive, more immediate and more vital than any set of beliefs. The doctrine of the Trinity is the carefully chosen frame that enables us to view the actual picture to best advantage. Some, like a myopic guide in a museum, have spent so much time talking about the frame that they have forgotten to point to the picture. Others, like people subjected to such nonsense, have concluded that if the frame is so boring the picture can't be worth looking at. But when, even for a moment, you just glimpse the picture – Isaiah's picture, Mark's picture, of the God whose scale dwarfs all our little maps – then you may find that the old frame does well enough, provided you use it as a frame should be used, that is, to let the picture itself be seen to best advantage.

And when you stand in front of this picture, the picture not of a strait-laced doctrine but of the humanized God, you realize, with Isaiah, that all geography, politics, religion, and astronomy is like so much stubble, like a bunch of twittering grasshoppers. God has to sweep away all our ideas, including all our ideas about God, in order to draw us, unwilling as we are, face to face with the reality, which is both greater and gentler than we can imagine. And if that is true in our praying and thinking – if it is true that we have to be stripped of our own noisy jumble of thoughts in order to hear afresh the word of the triune God – it is just as true in our living. We are summoned, again and again, to be found by God where he has promised to meet us, that is, in the wilderness.

It's lonely in the wilderness. Most of us aren't equipped for it. We like our world populated, and our creature comforts close at hand. Even when we choose solitude, we people it with books, music, and pictures; if we don't have them to hand, we retain them in our hearts. Most of us haven't even really begun to strip away the busyness and over-population of our mental furniture and to enter the wilderness, where, like Brian Keenan, we are alone, lonely, exposed, naked. But when we do find ourselves there, which may happen to any of us at any time, we find two figures to tell us the way. Isaiah and John the Baptist remind us that when we find ourselves in exile, at a loss, frightened, anxious beyond anxiety, crushed by our circumstances, our surroundings, our sin – then we are summoned to hear a fresh word of comfort. The doctrine of the Trinity is not meant to be part of a forbidding set of dogmas, however true those dogmas are. It is a doctrine of comfort; of healing and forgiveness; of waiting for the Lord, and discovering him to be, as we go out to face an unknown future, the one who gives power to the faint.

And we discover this God precisely as we look at Jesus. If Isaiah has given us a map of 'God on the same scale', Mark offers us a guide to the map; and more than a guide: one in whose face, in whose very self, the living and true God is present to save, to comfort, to strengthen. If you want to mount up with wings as eagles, you know what you have to do.

CHAPTER FIVE

The Glory of the Lord

He was a good man, and he had exhorted the people to
lead righteous lives, to practise justice towards their fel-
lows and piety towards God. When the crowds around
him began to increase, becoming extremely aroused by
his powerful preaching, the king became alarmed. Elo-
quence with such great effect might lead to rebellion.
The king therefore decided to strike first . . .

Those are the words of Josephus, the first-century Jewish
historian (*Antiquities* 18.116–18). The king was Herod
Antipas, the son of Herod the Great. The people were of
course the Jews, in or around AD 28. And the good man,
whose powerful preaching alarmed the king with the
thought of sedition, was of course John the Baptist, who
featured in our previous chapter.

The gospels' portrait of John the Baptist is filled out by
this quite independent account. Underneath the story we all
know, of Herod's dancing daughter and John's head on a
platter, we find the dark undercurrent of political fear. As
far as Herod was concerned, John was dangerous.

Well, of course he was. He was a voice, a voice that
would not be silent; a voice in the wilderness, a voice of
warning, a voice of promise, a voice in which some came
to believe they had heard the voice of God. Voices like that
are threatening to those with vested interests.

He was a different voice. He came from a priestly family, yet he was not himself living and working as a priest, but instead conducting a strange initiation ritual down by the Jordan. That very action, quite apart from anything he said, strongly implied that people could be true members of God's people, not by adherence to the Temple and the other Jewish symbols, but through his own work. Voices like that are worrying to those whose prestige is bound up with the current institutions.

He was a prophetic voice, in line with the prophets of old. Amos and Micah had warned the people about God's judgement falling on those who ignored basic principles of justice. Ezekiel and Jeremiah had predicted, and witnessed, the devastation of Jerusalem, as the people refused to heed their warnings. God had spoken through the prophets; and John, by his clothing, his food, and his habit of life seems to have been conscious of standing in that great and risky tradition. Risky, because kings tend not to like prophets. Voices that tell uncomfortable truths usually get silenced.

But what was the truth that John was telling? What was the message that was so urgent that he had to get it across even at the risk of his life? It was the news that all would be well at last; that the long night was nearly over, and that the day was about to break; that the God who had apparently abandoned his people was coming back: coming to rule, coming to judge, coming to save, coming to forgive. It was the Advent message.

It was, in other words, the message of Isaiah 40. This passage, which we were considering from a different angle earlier in this book, is one of the most memorable parts of the Old Testament; in our culture it has been made even more so by the fact that George Frederick Handel created no less than five pieces in his *Messiah* out of the first eleven verses alone. Handel starts where the chapter starts:

Comfort ye, comfort ye, my people
says your God;
Speak comfortably, tenderly, to Jerusalem,
and cry to her
that her warfare is accomplished, her iniquity pardoned;
that she has received from the LORD's hand
double for all her sins.

For the Jew in the first century the message would be
plain. The long night of exile is really over at last. Israel's
trials and tribulations at the hands of the pagans are coming
to an end. God has, somehow, dealt with her sin, the sin
because of which all her misery had come upon her. Now it
is time for comfort, for God to woo her again (when the
prophet says 'speak comfortably', or 'tenderly', he literally
says 'speak to her heart'; this is the language of wooing, of
engagement, of the tenderness and delicacy of gentle human
love). This is the first thing that we must stress, if we are
to understand Isaiah 40, and so to understand John the Baptist. Rough old John, with his camel-hair cloak and his
locusts and wild honey, seems an unlikely messenger to be
carrying God's love-letter to his forsaken and grieving
people, but that's the role he adopts. His is the message of
Advent, of the arrival of the Bridegroom – that is, of God
himself, coming at last to claim his bride and turn her waiting into dancing, her mourning into joy. This is exodus-
language. God will betroth Israel to himself once more, as
he did when he called her out of Egypt. This is why the
very creation itself must now get ready:

A voice cries,
'In the wilderness prepare the way of the LORD;
make straight in the desert a highway for our God.'
Every valley shall be lifted up,
and every mountain and hill be made low;

the uneven ground shall become level
and the rough places plain.

Why all this flattening out of the very surface of the earth? What's the big fuss? The answer – and this is the second thing that must be stressed – is that the Bridegroom is on his way home; God himself is returning to his people; and creation itself must roll out the red carpet to greet him. Then

the glory of the LORD shall be revealed;
and all flesh shall see it together;
for the mouth of the LORD has spoken it.

I suspect that when we read those words, or hear them sung by the choir in the first chorus of the *Messiah*, we don't at once see the picture. To get it right we would have to go back through the Old Testament to the passages which speak of the glory of the LORD being revealed. Sometimes this is in the Temple, as with Isaiah himself, and with Solomon when the Temple was first dedicated. But the most striking time is at the exodus, when Moses begs God to show him his glory, and God declines, revealing himself by hiding himself, letting Moses see only his back. Now we find the prophet declaring that in the wilderness, the exodus-place, God will at last reveal his full glory, his true glorious self; and not just to one or two favoured people, but to the whole world. 'All flesh shall see it together.' This is emphasized again a few verses later, in yet another piece that we can't read without thinking of George Frederick Handel:

Get up to a high mountain,
O herald of good tidings to Zion;
lift up your voice with strength,

lift it up, don't be afraid;
say to the cities of Judah
'Behold your God!'

What can all this mean, since, as the Old Testament stresses, no one can see God and live? And what can John the Baptist mean, by casting himself as the voice, the voice that cries, the herald whose words make the princelings tremble?

Our first thought is no doubt that the prophet envisaged God coming in, as we say, a blaze of glory. Perhaps he imagined that God would appear, shining like the sun, sitting on a throne or a chariot, surrounded by millions of angels. But we might begin to have some doubts about that. We have already discovered that the prophet speaks of God wooing his people gently, coming to them as a bridegroom to his bride. Appearing in blazing glory on a throne is hardly the way to speak to the heart of your beloved. And at the end of the passage, in yet another *Messiah* passage, we find this description of what God will do when he comes:

He will feed his flock like a shepherd,
he will gather the lambs in his arm,
he will carry them in his bosom,
and gently lead those that are with young.

Again, that's hardly the 'blaze of glory' that we might expect. How then is God going to appear?

The answer is the strangest thing you could think of. As we read on in Isaiah 40—55, we find that the coming of God focuses increasingly on the work of the Servant of the Lord. God will come to woo and win his people. But he will come, like the prince in the story, in the disguise of a beggar:

Who would have believed such news?
To whom has the Arm of the LORD been revealed?

He had no form or beauty that we should desire him;
[He did not come in a blaze of glory,
sweeping all before him,
with angels singing Hallelujah;]

He was despised and rejected by men,
a man of sorrows, and acquainted with grief.
Surely he has borne our griefs, and carried our sorrows;
he was wounded for our transgressions,
he was bruised for our iniquities;
the chastisement of our peace was upon him
and with his stripes we are healed.
All we like sheep have gone astray
we have turned every one to his own way;
and the LORD has laid on him the iniquity of us all.

We love these passages, and meditate on them each year as Holy Week comes round. But what we often fail to see is that, within their literary context, they form the climax of that great sustained passage of prophecy which purports to speak of how the living God returns to woo and win his people. What will it look like when God comes back to Jerusalem? Isaiah's answer is that it will not be a blaze of glory. It will not be in the form of a great military display of power. It will be in the life of one who takes upon himself the form of a servant, and is obedient unto death. This is how God will comfort his people; this is how the bridegroom will return to Zion; this is why Advent is good news, why we know that God is a shepherd who carries the lambs in his bosom, and gently leads those that are with young. To a world besotted with the love of power, Isaiah's God reveals himself in the power of love.

The Advent message, Isaiah's message for his hearers, is that this God is coming to judge the world by the law of love. There is always a danger that when we speak of God's judgment we imagine God as a fierce, bullying, domineering God. I suspect that many people in our society today, if they use the word 'God' at all (other than as an expletive), think of God basically like that. That's why so many of them have rejected him. There are quite enough fierce bullies in the world already without having one up in the sky as well. But the reason that the true God will come to right all wrongs in the world (and that's what 'judgment' really means) is not because he's a fierce bully but precisely because he is the bridegroom who wants to woo and win his bride; because he is the shepherd who longs to carry the lambs close to his heart; because he is the servant who is wounded for our transgressions and bruised for our iniquities. If this is what the true God is like, it's the fierce bullies – the Herods of the world – who are in for a shock. This is the God whose coming judgment will be based upon love. This is the God whose word will stand for ever, while the grass withers and the flower fades.

And what about old John, who cast himself in the role of the Voice that had to announce this Word, to herald the coming of this God? How much of all this did he understand?

Bits and pieces, I think. It is very revealing that, in the first chapter of John's gospel, he refuses to see himself as Elijah, let alone as the Messiah or the great final Prophet. He seems to have thought that Jesus was going to be Elijah; Jesus seems to have returned the compliment. Perhaps part of the strange vocation to be Elijah, to get the people ready for the coming of God, was precisely that one would not know the significance of one's own work. I suspect that a lot of vocation works like that. The only role John will accept, as we saw at the beginning, is that of the Voice: I am the voice of one crying in the wilderness, Make straight the way of the LORD. That is almost all he knows.

It is enough. Enough to create around him a community of the true Israel, on tiptoe with expectation for God to come and save and judge; a community among whom were people called Peter and Andrew, a community in whose midst there was one whose sandal-strap John was not worthy to untie. Enough to make Herod tremble on his throne at the thought that the old rumours of Israel's God coming back might after all be true, or at least that enough people might believe them to make life very difficult for his own shaky kingdom. Enough to challenge those who lived by the love of power with the old message, half-forgotten but never quite obliterated, of the power of love.

Enough, too, to challenge us in our own little kingdoms, and our own responsibilities. We, too, live on and live by the promised coming of God. We who live on the farther side of Christmas, Calvary, Easter and Pentecost stake our lives on the belief that, in the man Jesus, Isaiah's promise about the coming of the bridegroom to woo and win his people came true in literal human history. But if we believe that, we are also committed to the belief that this same God comes to us again week by week, in bread and wine, to woo and win us, to carry the lambs in his bosom, gently to lead the mother sheep. And we are committed to the belief that he will come again, finally, to judge and save his weary old world once and for all.

And our calling, therefore, as those who celebrate his strange and beautiful coming, is once again to be a voice. The church is here to be the Voice to the world; the Voice that does not claim great things for itself, but simply urges the world to get ready for the God who comes in the power and judgment of love. We are to live, and we are to speak, in such a way as to do for our generation, more or less, what John did for his: to demonstrate and to announce that there is a different way of being human, the way of love, the way of God, and so to bring to the world the news (good news for the weary, bad news for the bullies) that the creator of the world is also the comforter of the world:

Comfort ye, comfort ye, my people,
says your God;
speak comfortably to Jerusalem –
to London and Lichfield
to Birmingham and Bristol
to New York and Tokyo
to Rwanda and Bosnia
to Ireland
and, yes, to Jerusalem now as then;
and cry to her
that her warfare is accomplished
her iniquity is pardoned.
Prepare in the wilderness the way of the Lord;
make straight in the desert,
in the slum, in the high-rise,
in the swamp, in the battlefield,
in the palace, in the penthouse,
in the broken hearts of the world
a highway for our God.

CHAPTER SIX

The Face of Love

The scene is set in a prison cell. The prisoner, a man in early middle age, is writing a letter to a close friend. It's a tricky letter to write, because the friend has been very badly treated by a third party, and the prisoner, who has come to know the third party, is appealing for a reconciliation.

He makes two basic moves. First, he stresses the friendship which means that prisoner and free man are bonded together with ties of love: you and I belong together, he says, as one. In the same breath, he stresses that he and the third party have also become very close, like father and son. The friend, reading thus far, discovers that if he values the prisoner's friendship, he is going to have to take the wrongdoer along with him. Then, second, he faces the question of the wrongdoing itself. All right, he says, there has been trouble; but whatever it was, I want you to put it down to my account, not his. Blame me for it; I'll repay you any damages he owes you. And by the end of the letter the friend really has no choice. He is faced with sheer love; and he would have to have a stony heart indeed not to respond as the prisoner indicates.

In case you haven't recognized him, the prisoner is of course St Paul; the friend is Philemon; the wrongdoer is the runaway slave Onesimus. The prison is probably in Ephesus, on the Turkish coast, about a hundred miles from

Philemon's home in Colosse, up the Lycus valley. And I want to suggest to you that if the little letter from Paul to Philemon, one of the shortest books in the New Testament, was the only scrap of evidence that we had about early Christianity, we would still have to conclude that something very remarkable had happened in the first century which had radically changed the way people looked at themselves, at one another, and at the world.

There are other letters in antiquity which speak about runaway slaves and similar problems. Normally they adopt a patronizing and condescending tone: the slave or equivalent is of course irrelevant, scarcely human, but, my dear fellow, you might want to show what a good chap you are and give the rascal a second chance. (That would be at the most generous end of the scale.) Paul's letter breathes a totally different air. He and Philemon are brothers in Christ. He and Onesimus are brothers in Christ. Paul stands between the two of them, with both arms outstretched, to embrace and unite both master and slave. He becomes, in himself, the bond of love that will unite them. He becomes the place where, and the means by which, the pain and anger and guilt of their relationship is snuffed out and dealt with.

Paul would have seen, better than we do, the significance of the posture: a human being with arms outstretched, bearing the shame and the pain, and effecting healing and reconciliation. This is a new idea, and much more than an idea, a new fact, a new way of being, a new force let loose in the world. And where it comes from is quite clear. It comes from Calvary, where Pontius Pilate's most famous prisoner stretched out his arms to embrace Jew and Greek, slave and free, male and female; and, beyond that, to embrace and reconcile God and humanity, the creator and his runaway slave, the creator and his runaway world. Paul gives us our earliest written evidence of the first and, in a sense, the main thing I want to say in this chapter: that the cross of Jesus *changed the world*.

And I want to say this particularly in order to guard against the belittling of the cross which can so easily creep in to our thinking, and even to our praying and our devotion. The cross of Jesus is such a huge reality, standing in the middle of the world and of history, that we are often at a loss to know how to respond to it, what we're supposed to think or do when we're confronted with it. When we try to say that the cross means this, or that, or the other thing, we usually end up doing something analogous to playing a Beethoven symphony on a mouth-organ. We bring it down to the level of our own thinking and feeling, instead of allowing it to lift our thinking and feeling – yes, and our praying and living and loving – up to its own level.

I don't pretend for a moment that what I say here will escape the same problem. But I want to try to point beyond words, including my own words, so that our eyes rest on the fact itself. And the fact is, as I say, that the cross of Jesus *changed the world*. It didn't just create a new possibility for human devotion. It didn't just reveal an aspect of the character of God. It wasn't just the most wonderful example of a terrible death bravely suffered. It changed the world.

How, more particularly? The cross and resurrection of Jesus didn't just happen at some miscellaneous moment in the past. They came as the culmination of a long history, in which the creator God had been preparing his great plan for the saving of his world. The time is fulfilled, said Jesus, and now at last God is becoming King. When the time had fully come, said Paul, God sent forth his Son to redeem the world. Jesus' life, and supremely his death, simply don't make sense if we see them as the action of one man standing in the middle of nowhere. They only make sense when seen as the climax of the creator's plan to save the world.

In particular, they only make sense if we understand the plight of the world in its most radical form. Those who have looked most deeply into the face of this world's evil have regularly concluded that evil is something more than simply the sum total of individual acts of wrongdoing. Evil exerts a destructive power which goes beyond even those who implement it. Pontius Pilate was a little man swept along by the tradition and ethos of a ruthless empire. Annas and Caiaphas were little men who happened to be at the leading edge of a two-thousand-year-old national way of life. Herod was a little man who held on to power in the way that little men do, by blustering and bullying. Even the emperor Tiberius, brooding back in Rome, was only ultimately a little man. Something bigger than all of them was at work; and that something was decisively challenged by the one person of all time who was not a little man; the man who had grasped a secret which the world's rulers never knew, that to be great you must be the slave of all, that the power of love is stronger than the love of power.

And the result was inevitable. They did to him what they often did to runaway slaves: they crucified him. He took upon himself, literally and historically, the force and weight of the evil systems of the world, that reveal their evil nature by crushing human beings, human freedom, human love. It is not merely a theological or spiritual truth that Jesus bore the sin of the world: on the first Good Friday, it was politically and historically true. That is why it changed the world.

The truth of the cross is therefore bigger than, and logically prior to, all our devotion, all our sense of pity and awe and wonder at the suffering of the Son of God. If it were not, our keeping of Good Friday would become roughly the same sort of thing as the horror and sympathy we feel when confronted with Rwanda, or Sarajevo, or Dunblane. Good Friday transcends that level, important though it is in itself. It is about the moment when the principalities and powers over-reached themselves. As Paul says in another letter, the powers that run the world didn't understand what they were doing when they crucified the Lord of Glory. Pride, greed, fear, arrogance and ultimately violence stay in circulation because when they operate they create more of themselves: one person's pride begets another person's jealousy, one act of violence begets another. In this case, the pride and fear and violence of all the world – the greatest empire the world had ever seen, the highest religion the world had ever known – did their worst to Jesus. And he prayed, 'Father, forgive them; they don't know what they're doing.' And, in dying without bitterness, without pride, without retaliation, he changed the world. He acted out the victory of love over evil.

Ah but, you say, the world isn't changed. Pride and violence still exist. We are still subject to them – even we who believe in Jesus. At this point it would be easy to say: yes, well, but Jesus has opened up the possibility for men and women to live in a different way, and our task as individuals is to do so as best we can. No doubt that is true, so far as it goes.

But the cross, as expounded in the New Testament, speaks of a victory that goes deeper than that. Just as evil is more than the sum total of individual acts of wrongdoing, so Jesus' victory over evil is more than the sum total of subsequent individual acts of selfless love. Christian faith, faith in the crucified Jesus, is more than my individual belief that he died for me, vital though that is. It is the faith that on the cross Jesus in principle won the victory over sin, violence, pride, arrogance and even death itself, *and that that victory can now be implemented*. This faith refuses to accept that violence, greed and pride are unassailable and unchallengeable. This faith will go to work to challenge and subvert those destructive forces, in ourselves, in our local communities, in our corporate and political life, in the belief, albeit often in the teeth of the evidence, that they have been defeated and that the power of God's love is stronger than they are. To say that the cross changed the world is a statement of faith; but it is not blind faith, whistling in the dark. It is faith that looks up at the creator God and knows him to be the God of love. And it is faith that looks out at the world with the longing to bring that love to bear in healing, reconciliation, and hope.

You see, if the cross of Jesus changed the world, there is a sense in which, also, the cross of Jesus *changed God*. Now don't misunderstand me. I'm not saying (though some have said it) that prior to the cross God was an angry, vindictive tyrant, and that after the cross he became a loving father once again. Those two great theologians of the cross, Paul and John, both insist that the cross was an action from God's own side, an act of the greatest and deepest love. The cross, from that point of view, reveals what was always true: that God so loved the world, that God was in Christ reconciling the world to himself. Yes, but in the process, if we may so speak, God *became* on the cross what God always was. I may have it in me, in ability and desire, to climb Mount Everest; but until I actually go into training and do it it remains latent. You may have it in you to be a brilliant concert pianist; but until you get down to practice and performance, all that brilliance remains latent. God always was the God of love – generous, spontaneous, free and cheerful self-giving love; but until God, if we dare put it like this, gets down to practice and performance, that love at its deepest level remains latent. On the cross God at last performs the score composed before the foundation of the world. On the cross God at last scales the highest of the peaks. It isn't just that the cross *reveals* God's love in the most striking way. It reveals it because it *enacts* it. It becomes part of, indeed the most central part of, the personal history of God. God becomes the prisoner in the condemned cell, writing in his own blood the letter of reconciliation.

And so, as at creation God worked for six days, completing on the Friday the loving and generous work of creation, and resting on the seventh day, the Saturday, so on Good Friday God finally completes the loving and generous work he had set himself to accomplish. The last chord dies away, and the pianist leaves the keyboard, exhausted. The sun goes down on the mountain, and the mountaineer is taken home, totally spent. The letter is sent, and does its work, even as the prisoner is led away to the gallows. God rested in the tomb on the seventh day, the great Holy Saturday, the time of stillness, when passion and compassion had done their work, had completed their task. He had at last become what he always was: the world's true lover.

And now, to all eternity, the cross remains at the heart of God, stands as the truest symbol of God, offers the most exact and precise exposition of God. Part of the point of the doctrine of the Trinity is that what happened to Jesus of Nazareth on the first Good Friday happened to God; and, having happened to God, it has, so to speak, made God decisively and in practice, once and for all, what he always was in principle. That is why, on Good Friday, those who come to church do so, not to venerate a piece of wood (that, after all, would be the grossest pagan folly), but to use the cross as the truest possible icon of the living and loving God. As with any icon, the point is to look through it at the reality, of which, like all true symbols, the cross speaks more deeply than words.

And, as we look, and worship, it is not only the world that is changed; it is not only God who is changed; *we ourselves are changed*. We are changed, after all, by a smile from a stranger; how can we not be changed when we look at the face of Love himself? We find ourselves caught and held in the outstretched arms of the divine prisoner; we are captivated by the music of his stretched sinews; we are swept up to the mountain-tops, from which we see the whole world in a new way. And we ourselves, made prisoners in our turn by that love, discover that we have a new identity. As we are set free by that love from our own pride and fear, our own greed and arrogance, so we are free in our turn to be agents of reconciliation and hope, of healing and love. We are to be the prisoners who will write the letter; we are to reach out to God and the world and hold them together in our own very selves, our own actions, our own words, our own lives. This is what praying for the world is all about. This is what Christian political action is all about. This is what visiting the sick and dying is all about. This is what marriage counselling is all about. It is what being a Christian in the thousands of walks of life to which we are called is all about.

And none of this is dreamed up, or drummed up, by our own effort or will-power. It follows from, and flows from, the fact that the cross of Jesus changed the world once and for all, and that since Calvary the creator of the world has been known by the symbol of the cross.

And as we engage in this cross-shaped ministry of reconciliation, we must not be surprised if from time to time it feels as though we ourselves are being pulled apart. We talk of 'taking up the cross' or 'having a cross to bear' as though God somewhat arbitrarily gave each of us some pain or trouble just to make things difficult for us, to stop us having too easy a life of it. Not so. Just as evil is more than the sum total of human wrongdoing, and just as God's victory over evil is more than the sum total of subsequent human loving, so our ministry of reconciliation is more than simply the words we speak and the physical acts we perform. We ourselves, as whole persons, are caught up in the process in ways beyond our understanding, so that our suffering, whatever it may be, becomes part of Christ's own passion, of God's own passion, and as such brings healing and reconciliation at levels and depths beyond our imagining. Our task is to be faithful to the calling of the cross: to live in God's new world as the agents of his love, and to pray that the cross we carry today will become part of the healing and reconciliation of the world. We will not understand in the present time how it is that our pain, our illness, our heartbreak, our deep frustration, is somehow taken up into the pain of God and the healing of the world; but if we offer it back to God that is precisely what will happen.

What we do on Good Friday, therefore, is more than the fuelling of private devotion, though it should be that as well. It is more than the learning of some theological truths, though it is vital to do that also. It is looking into the face of Love, that we may reflect that Love into the world. It is allowing ourselves to be changed into the image of the God who was himself changed on Calvary, so that the world which was decisively changed on the first Good Friday may finally be changed until it reflects the love, the justice and the peace which met and embraced on the cross. It is learning the meaning of life from the condemned prisoner. It is discovering reconciliation in the outstretched arms of God.

CHAPTER SEVEN

No Bones About It

On Palm Sunday 1996 the *Sunday Times* ran a feature about the tomb of Jesus. At least, it was supposed to be about Jesus' tomb; but actually nobody made the claim explicit. There were, predictably, some misleading headlines. Some suggested that the discovery threatened the basis of Christianity. One spoke of 'The tomb that dare not speak its name' – which was silly, because that was precisely what the tomb did, which was why there was a story at all. Other newspapers got in on the act. The radio stations chattered away about it all week.

What happened was this. Two BBC producers went looking for fresh material for the Easter Sunday edition of the programme *The Heart of the Matter*. They wanted to stimulate discussion on the nature of the resurrection. Supposing, they wanted to ask, someone actually found the bones of Jesus lying around in Palestine: what would that do to Christian faith? So they looked for ossuaries – bone-boxes. They found one that said 'Jesus, son of Joseph' (actually, they found more than one, but they only followed one up). It had been found in a family tomb; and in the same family tomb were other boxes, labelled Joseph, Mary, another Mary, a Matthew, and someone called Judah, described as 'the son of Jesus'. Actually, the boxes were empty: vandals had apparently got there first, possibly in antiquity. There were, so to speak, no bones about it. But journalists are good at putting two and two together and making seventeen. Could this be Jesus' tomb? Would it cast doubt on the very foundations of Christianity?

The first thing to say is that, even if nobody had ever said Jesus of Nazareth had been raised to life, the probability is still enormously high that this would not have been the tomb of the Jesus, Mary and Joseph we know from the gospels. 'Mary' is by far the most common female name in the period; 'Joseph' and 'Jesus' are two of the most common male names, with Judah – or Judas – not far behind. So discovering a tomb with these names in one family is rather like someone coming across an English tombstone with a Tom, Dick and Harry all in the same family. Or, more sharply, it's like an archaeologist two thousand years hence finding an English tomb with parents called Philip and Elizabeth and children called Charles and Anne, and claiming that this must be the British royal family. The Israeli archaeologists, none of them interested in defending Christianity, were the first to pooh-pooh the idea of this being the tomb of Jesus of Nazareth.

The second thing to say is that, if it had been the tomb of Jesus and his family, there are serious oddities. Why is it in Jerusalem, when the family lived in Nazareth, where (presumably) Joseph had died some time before Jesus' public ministry? Why is there no mention of James, Jesus' most famous brother, or of Joses and Simon (as listed in Mark 6.3, along with some unnamed sisters)? And why on earth is there a *son* of Jesus? There is no evidence whatever that Jesus had children, whether in or out of wedlock; and we need to remind ourselves that his family – that is, his brothers and nephews – were well known in the early church. Sixty years after Jesus' death, his great-nephews were accused by the Roman emperor Domitian of being part of a would-be royal family. If Jesus had had a son, people would have known. It would have mattered.

But the most serious problem is yet to come – and this points forward to the real message of Easter, which I want to focus on here. Bone-boxes, ossuaries, were used in the *second* stage of a two-stage burial process. Many first-century Jews were buried this way. First they were laid on a slab, wrapped in cloth with spices. The tomb was a cave, not a hole in the ground. It would have a movable stone door; the family and friends would in due course lay other bodies on other shelves in the same cave. Then, a year or more later, when all the flesh had decomposed, relatives or friends would return to collect the bones and place them in an ossuary, a box roughly two feet by one foot by one foot, which would then be stored away either in recesses within the same cave or somewhere else. In other words, the burial of Jesus as recorded in the gospels was only the first stage of an intended *two*-stage burial.

So: did anyone ever think of going back to the tomb to collect Jesus' bones and put them in an ossuary? No, they didn't! The whole early church knew that Jesus' body wasn't in the tomb. They believed that God had raised Jesus to life again, transforming his body in the process. This wasn't a resuscitation, a journey back into the present life; it was a resurrection, a going on through death and out the other side into a new mode of physicality, the beginning of God's new creation. If the disciples had believed that what they called the 'resurrection' was just (what we would call) a 'spiritual' event, leaving the body in the tomb, someone sooner or later would have had to go back to collect Jesus' bones and store them properly. They couldn't and wouldn't have left a skeleton just lying there on the ledge, with only the first stage of burial complete. The tomb was designed, like most such tombs of the period, as a family tomb. As further family members died, the relatives would in due course have come again with their bodies, to lay them elsewhere in the tomb. The ledge where

Jesus had been laid would be needed again. But of course, if anyone had at any stage gone back to tidy up Jesus' bones and put them in an ossuary, that would indeed have destroyed Christianity before it had even properly begun. Even those contemporary scholars who deny that Jesus was raised bodily from the dead are clear that all the early Christians thought he had been, and that they made it the basis of their whole life.

So the question of the ossuaries, when we explore it thoroughly, provides paradoxically a sort of negative evidence in favour of Jesus' resurrection. Not only is the tomb the journalists are highlighting not Jesus' tomb. By drawing attention to the two-stage burial process, they have reminded us of how impossible it is to imagine Christianity getting off the ground at all if the second stage of the burial process had ever been carried out. Make no bones about it. In their eagerness to find news, the journalists have accidentally highlighted the good news.

You see, belief in Jesus' resurrection was never simply belief in a life after death. Someone on a radio show in Holy Week, after the original article, declared that it didn't matter if Jesus' bones were still lying around Palestine somewhere, because, he said, 'I expect to go to heaven when I die, and I won't be taking my bones with me; so I don't see why Jesus shouldn't have done the same.' I suspect that that idea, or something like it, is quite widespread, and it's worth pointing out the mistake. Belief in Jesus' resurrection is *not* the belief that Jesus has simply 'gone to heaven' after his death, as though Jesus were like a great saint or martyr whom God has received into his presence with honour. Jews believed that about all sorts of people; it wouldn't have been new; it wouldn't have been *news*. Easter faith always was the belief that Jesus went through death into a new sort of bodily existence, in which his original body was transformed into a body with new characteristics and properties. When St Paul, the first Christian to write about the resurrection, draws conclusions from Jesus' resurrection to ours, he says that those who are still alive at the end of time will have their bodies *changed*. He talks about seeds and plants, about acorns and oaks. Our bodies won't be abandoned; they will be transformed. That is what Paul, in common with all other early Christians, thought had happened to Jesus.

So what was the resurrection all about, as far as the early Christians were concerned? And what on earth – and I mean *on earth* – does it mean for the world and the church at the end of the twentieth century?

The early Christians very quickly came to understand what had happened to Jesus in terms of the old Jewish, biblical belief that the living God was one day going to solve the problem of Israel's exile and oppression, and by doing so was going to solve the problem of evil and injustice in the whole world. That is what it means to say that the resurrection took place 'according to the scriptures': it was the fulfilment of prophetic promises and long-cherished hopes. Putting it crudely, the resurrection demonstrated that the cross was a victory, not a defeat. As St Paul says, if Christ is not raised, your faith is futile, and you are still in your sins. But if Christ has been raised, then this shows that on the cross he defeated death, and hence sin, and hence all evil and injustice, once and for all. Easter isn't just about one person going through death and out the other side, as a sort of crazy maverick event unrelated to anything else, a sort of one-off display of supernatural power. It is the unveiling of God's answer to the problems of the world.

You see, just as that early Christian belief in the resurrection of Jesus was a belief about something that actually happened within this real world, not simply a belief about a transcendent dimension, a spiritual or other-worldly reality which leaves this world behind, so the continuing message of the resurrection is precisely *not* that 'there is a life after death'. There is, and all God's people will inherit it; but the point is that it won't be what most modern Westerners think of as 'life after death'. It will involve God's people being given new bodies, like Jesus' body, to share in the new heavens *and new earth* that God will make. The message of the resurrection is that this present world matters; that the problems and pains of this present world matter; that the living God has made a decisive bridgehead into this present world with his healing and all-conquering love; and that, in the name of this strong love, all the evils, all the injustices and all the pains of the present world must now be addressed with the news that healing, justice and love have won the day. That's why we pray 'Thy Kingdom come, *on earth as it is in heaven*'. Make no bones about it: Easter Day was the first great answer to that prayer.

You see, if Easter faith is simply about believing that God has a nice comfortable after-life for some or all of us, then Christianity becomes a mere pie-in-the-sky religion instead of a kingdom-on-earth-as-it-is-in-heaven religion. Or, if Easter faith is simply about believing that Jesus is risen in some 'spiritual' sense, leaving his body in the tomb, then Christianity turns into a let-the-world-stew-in-its-own-juice religion, instead of a kingdom-on-earth-as-it-is-in-heaven religion. If Easter faith is only about me, and perhaps you, finding a new dimension to our own personal spiritual lives in the here and now, then Christianity becomes simply a warmth-in-the-heart religion, instead of a kingdom-on-earth-as-it-is-in-heaven religion. It becomes focused on me and my survival, my sense of God, my spirituality, rather than outwards on God, and on God's world that still needs the kingdom-message so badly. But if Jesus Christ is truly risen from the dead, Christianity becomes what the New Testament insists that it is: good news for the whole world, news which warms our hearts *precisely because it isn't just about warming hearts*. The living God has in principle dealt with evil once and for all, and is now at work, by his own Spirit, to do for us and the whole world what he did for Jesus on that first Easter day.

That is why we who celebrate Easter do so with material things: water (not least when people are baptized at an Easter vigil, as in the ancient Christian custom); bread and wine at the Eucharist. Easter is about the living God claiming the world of space, time and matter as his own. That is why Christians celebrate it with candles and flowers and incense and processions and banners and, above all, music: the world of creation has been reclaimed by the living and healing God. That is why we who celebrate Easter after a Lenten fast do so not with a guilty sense of going back to things that are tainted with sin, but with the joyful sense of celebrating the goodness of God's good creation in all its rich variety. That is why the celebration of Easter calls us, one and all, to delight in God's way of holiness: not a negative, gloomy holiness, but a positive giving of ourselves to God in the knowledge that his way is the way of true delight, of true fulfilment. And that is why the celebration of Easter, in a world, a country, and a region where injustice, violence, degradation and all manner of wickedness are still endemic, makes the most powerful symbolic statement that we are not prepared to tolerate such things – that God is not prepared to tolerate such things – and that we will work, and plan, and pray, and vote, with all the energy of God to implement the victory of Jesus over them all. True Easter faith, true Easter celebration, and true Easter holiness, must issue in true Easter agendas. Let's make no bones about it.

You see, the old jibe of Karl Marx and others that Christianity lulls people into being content with their lot, and content to look on other people's misery and injustice, because it speaks only about a spiritualized heaven in the future and a spiritual experience here and now – that jibe is a fair critique of that watered-down Christianity which tries to say that Jesus' body, like John Brown's, stayed a-mouldering in the grave while his soul went marching on. But it misses entirely the point of the true Christian belief in the resurrection. Here's an interesting thing: notice how, in the gospels, all the first witnesses of the resurrection *run*. Half the references in the gospels to people running occur in the resurrection stories: the women run *from* the tomb, Peter and John run *to* the tomb, the disciples in Emmaus hurry back to Jerusalem. Where is that energy in the church today, a god-given energy that can't wait to get the good news out and to implement it in the world? If it is lacking, could it have something to do with the fact that far too many Christians have been lulled into thinking that God isn't really concerned with this world, so that the resurrection of Jesus isn't about something happening within this world, so that the only thing that matters is my private other-worldly salvation?

You see, the bodily resurrection of Jesus isn't a take-it-or-leave-it thing, as though some Christians are welcome to believe it and others are welcome not to believe it. Take it away, and the whole picture is totally different. Take it away, and Karl Marx was probably right to accuse Christianity of ignoring the problems of the material world. Take it away, and Sigmund Freud was probably right to say that Christianity is a wish-fulfilment religion. Take it away, and Friedrich Nietzsche was probably right to say that Christianity was a religion for wimps. Put it back, and you have a faith that can take on the postmodern world that looks to Marx, Freud and Nietzsche as its prophets, and you can beat them at their own game with the Easter news that the foolishness of God is wiser than men, and the weakness of God is stronger than men.

Those who celebrate the mighty resurrection of the Lord Jesus Christ, therefore, have an awesome and non-negotiable responsibility. When we say 'Alleluia! Christ is Risen', we are saying that Jesus is Lord of the world, and that the present would-be lords of the world are not. When we sing, in the old hymn, that 'Judah's Lion burst his chains, and crushed the serpent's head', are we ready to put that victory into practice? Are we ready to stand alongside our fellow Christians, even in civilized Britain, whose churches are regularly desecrated and vandalized? Are we ready to speak up for, and to take action on behalf of, those even in our own local community, let alone further afield, who are quietly being crushed by uncaring and unjust systems? Are we ready to speak up for the truth of the gospel over the dinner-table, and in the coffee-bar, and in the council-chamber? Let's make no bones about it: if Easter isn't good news, then there is no good news. But if it is – if it is true that Jesus Christ is risen indeed – then Easter day, and the Easter message, is the true sun which, when it rises, puts all other suns to shame:

> The sunne arising in the East,
> Though he give light, and th' East perfume,
> If they should offer to contest
> With Thy arising, they presume.
>
> Can there be any day but this,
> Though many sunnes to shine endeavour?
> We count three hundred, but we misse:
> There is but one, and that one ever.

> (George Herbert, 'Easter: The Song')

Part Two: Reflecting God's Image in the World

CHAPTER EIGHT

Remember

When *The Lord of the Rings* was first published, at least one reviewer accused its author, J. R. R. Tolkien, of writing 'escapist' literature. 'All right,' replied Tolkien, 'who is it who doesn't want people to escape? I'll tell you: *Gaolers*.' It's a good answer: but will it do for us? Here we are, with parts of the world ripping themselves apart in sectarian or ethnic violence; here we are, with the nameless horrors of civil wars being flashed on to our television screens from other parts of the global village; here we are, with wars and rumours of wars all round the globe, cheerfully kept going by those in our own civilized countries who supply them with weapons. We, for our part, when we want, officially as it were, to remember wars and rumours of wars, put on paper poppies and sing magnificent Magnificats. What do we say to the charge of 'escapism'? How do we answer the voices singing in our ears, as Eliot said of the Wise Men, insisting that this is all folly?

Let's go back to the book of Exodus. Moses had run away and escaped. He had cherished the dream of freedom for the captive Israelites. He had begun the process by killing an Egyptian. It hadn't worked; he was in deep trouble, and he left town fast. His instant solution had just made matters worse. But while he was in the wilderness, living as a shepherd, the plight of the Israelites became so appalling that they cried to their God in their misery; and, we are told, God heard their cry, and God *remembered* the covenant he had made with Abraham, Isaac and Jacob. Our remembering often turns into nostalgia or recrimination; God's remembering turns into action. The next thing we know, Moses is standing before a bush, a desert shrub. The bush is on fire, but the fire is not burning the bush.

Moses had heard about God before. He had even tried to act on behalf of God before. Now he finds himself in the presence of God, and suddenly everything looks rather different. Moses, like Adam in front of another tree, is afraid and hides. But the God who is revealed as fire is not to be escaped. He has words to speak to Moses, words which tell of his great compassion for his suffering people, words full of hope and promise and covenant love. And Moses is called to stand in awe before the beauty and power and majesty of God – in order that he may then stand without fear before the pomp and might of Pharaoh, king of Egypt, and in the name of the one true God demand the release of the true people of God.

Later on in the story we are told that Moses was very *meek*. Don't misunderstand that; the word 'meek' doesn't mean 'weak'. It's the word you'd use of a wild horse that's been tamed. Young man Moses, charging off to do God's will, killing the Egyptian: there's the wild horse, worse than useless. Mature Moses, standing before Pharaoh: he doesn't even have to raise his voice. There's the wild horse, tamed. The secret of the difference is what happened at the burning bush, where Moses stood and trembled in the very presence of the living God.

Moses, then, had escaped into the wilderness, away from the problem. But he hadn't escaped from God. And when we widen the angle again, and see the whole story of which the burning bush is a part, we see what was going on. Moses met God at the bush *because* God had heard the cry of his people and had remembered his promises; and he met God at the bush *in order that* God could call him to be his agent in putting those promises into effect. His earlier failure was not just overlooked. It was actually part of the training. Moses already knew that there was a wrong way of going about setting people free. He was now to discover the right way, by listening to the voice that came from inside the fire.

I want now to suggest that Western society has got to the same stage that Moses had got to when he found he had to leave Egypt in a hurry; that what our society desperately needs is a fresh vision of the living God; and that what we do when we come to worship, so far from being escapism, is actually designed to fuel and fire that vision. Vision without action would indeed be escapism; action without vision is blundering folly. We have a fair amount of both in the church and the world at the moment, perhaps more of the latter (action without vision) than the former. When God remembers his promises, though, he will act through people whose actions are grounded in vision, the burning vision of his saving covenant love.

First, then, where we've got to as a society. We haven't lost all moral sense, as some would say. Ours is in fact a very moralistic age: consider the sheer moral fury of those who protest about (for instance) fox-hunting. It's just that we've changed the moral targets. People who would be horrified to have an older sexual morality imposed on them 'for their own good' are eager to impose a new ecological morality on others 'for their own good'. This is a recipe for moral confusion, and there's plenty of that about right now.

Take some examples. We are all passionately in favour of justice, but somehow it slips through our fingers. We all long for peace in the world, but nobody quite knows how to achieve it. When we did decide to do something, as in the Gulf War, we ended up protecting and liberating some of the most oppressive regimes in the world, while leaving the Kurds to freeze in the mountains, and the Shiites to be gassed in the marshes. Since the collapse of the Berlin Wall, which had at least provided us with the illusion that we knew how the world was to be run, with a fatally easy goodies-and-baddies analysis, the West has looked suspiciously like Moses, doing the right thing for the wrong reason, the wrong thing for the right reason, and, as often as not, the wrong thing for the wrong reason. And, all over the Western world, people are asking where on earth we go from here.

Meanwhile, the cry of the poor gets louder. And if the living God heard the cry of his people in Egypt three and a half thousand years ago, he surely hears the cry that rises now from the bereaved in Belfast, the dispossessed in Palestine, the starving in the Sudan, and those in Bosnia and elsewhere who face another winter of freezing homes and hospitals, of battered and shattered lives. And if God hears this cry, and remembers his promise that the wolf shall lie down with the lamb, that swords will be beaten into ploughshares, that the whole earth will be filled with his glory, his justice and his peace, then how is he going to act? What is he going to do? When God remembers his promises, his memory moves him to action: as the Red Queen said, it's a poor memory that only works backwards. But God's way of action, now as then, is through a people, maybe even through an individual, who have glimpsed a fresh vision of his fire, and have heard for themselves his words of promise. They will almost certainly be unlikely people. Like Moses, they won't be expecting it. They may well not want it. But if they will only stand in fear before the living and burning God, they will be enabled to stand without fear before the Pharaohs of today.

So where do we learn to stand in fear before this God? In our worship. Many movements in the modern church try to make the worship of God more accessible; often all they succeed in doing is to trivialize it. Of course there must be understanding, of a sort, if worship is not to degenerate into mumbo-jumbo. But when you are confronted by fire, the proper response is not rational analysis, or 'will-the-people-in-the-pew-understand-it?', or a lowest-common-denominator levelling of words or music, but falling on your face. And, without mincing any words, people are more likely to be confronted by the majesty and awesomeness of God when the music and drama used in worship was written and is performed with that in mind.

This, to be sure, places an awesome responsibility on the musicians and liturgical organizers. Church music is meant to be a polished silver chalice, in which the strong wine of God's love is given to the rest of us. It is meant to be a burnished brazier which allows the congregation to warm themselves at God's fire. Woe betide, of course, the chalice or brazier that forgets what it is there for; but woe betide those who scoff at the polish or the burnishing because they cannot see what lies within. There is, after all, no escape from the temptation to professionalism: those whose churches eschew traditional choirs, and are filled instead with sound-systems and electronic gadgets, still need their professionals, who concentrate on their microphones and switches, as traditional choirs and organists concentrate on their minims and crotchets, so that the others may worship unhindered. No: what matters is that in worship we should enter the presence of the living God. And the music, if it is appropriate, can be a vital element in that awesome event.

But we meet with the high and holy one, the God of

fire, in order that we may ourselves be transformed and be his agents for the healing of his world. The God we worship is the God who hears the cry of his people, who remembers his promises, and who therefore desires to act not only for us but also through us. To enjoy worship for its own sake, or simply out of a cultural appreciation of the 'performance' (whether of Byrd or heavy rock), would be like Moses coming upon a burning bush and deciding to cook his lunch on it. No: we too need to cultivate a memory that works forwards as well as backwards. We remember, with due solemnity, events in the past which have shaped our national, social and personal life. But, as we do so in the presence of the living God, we must listen also for the voice which says: 'I have heard the cry of my people; and so I am sending *you* to *Pharaoh.*' We are not escapists, when we come to worship the true God and to pray for his bruised and bleeding world. On the contrary. We come so that, in whatever ways God calls us, small or great, we can be his agents in rescuing the world that still lies in gaol and cries for freedom. We, after all, stand before a yet more glorious tree: the tree of Calvary, which speaks, more truly than any words, of the fire of love which still burns at the heart of the living God.

CHAPTER NINE

Doing What He Was Told

He was only doing what he was told, after all.

One of the oldest tricks in the bureaucratic book is to tax people when they move from place to place. In Vancouver international airport you buy your ticket, you check your bags, you go through Customs, and then, when you think you're clear, you pass another little booth where they take a further ten dollars' airport tax off you. (This was true in 1995; I hope they soon scrap the system, if they haven't already.) Of course by then you're committed to travelling, and what's ten dollars compared with the price of the ticket? So you grumble inwardly and you pay up outwardly.

It can't be much fun to be the person collecting that ten dollars from thousands of people every day. You're on the receiving end of the veiled anger – and sometimes not so veiled – of those who feel it's a bit of a con. It's a bit like being a traffic warden. Or a prison warder. But there it is. It's their job. They're only doing what they're told.

Now if they'd had aeroplanes in the first century, you can be quite sure they'd have had an airport tax. One of the reasons Herod the Great could afford to rebuild the Temple in Jerusalem (here's something I bet you didn't know) was because he built a new harbour and forced all sea traffic to go through it, paying him a tax for the privilege. But when Herod the Great died, around the time Jesus was born, he divided his large kingdom between his sons. What does dividing a kingdom mean, when it comes to airport taxes or their ground-level equivalent? It means a lot more of them. Imagine if you had to pay a toll every time you crossed a county boundary while travelling around Britain. You'd think twice before driving fifty miles.

And where did you pay these taxes in Jesus' day? Not on the border itself; it would be dangerous to have a little booth stuck out by itself miles away from anywhere. No; the tax collection centre was in the first town you would come to once you'd crossed the border. After the death of Herod the Great, the northern part of his kingdom was divided between Philip and Antipas, east and west; and if you travelled west, from Philip's territory to Antipas', you would cross the border by crossing the Jordan just above the Sea of Galilee. And the first town you would come to on the western side was Capernaum. And in Capernaum there would be waiting for you a man called Levi ben Alphaeus, with a fixed smile and an outstretched hand. And you would think much the same thoughts as people think today in Vancouver international airport; only you would think them somewhat more bitterly, because you would know that Levi, Alphie's boy, made his living on the mark-up he chose to set between what he was supposed to charge and what he actually charged. And he would know that you would know. And you would know that he would know that you would know. And so on.

He was only doing his job.

But think what it does to you on the inside, if you're putting on that fixed smile six days a week, fifty weeks a year, allowing for Passover and the odd other holiday. It's not a great way to be a human being. It does things to you. It shows on your face. It shows in your voice, the superficial politeness with the threat of anger lurking underneath. It probably shows at home, with your wife and children.

And the trouble is that Levi, Alphie's boy, may well not have wanted very much to be a toll collector. The system needed someone, and found him. And so the social isolation, the cold shoulder from polite society, was probably reflected in the way he felt about himself. Because he had to get on with the job, he probably didn't very often confront the way he felt about himself. That does things to you, too. It's remarkable how many people are frightened of looking inside themselves, because of what they suspect they'll find. And if I'd been Levi, Alphie's son, I'd have been frightened of doing that, too.

Now we have to do all that ancient history, and all that amateur psychology, simply in order to get on the map of the story of Levi (Mark 2.13-17). Mark's first readers would have known all of that in their bones with the very first sentence. They would have seen instinctively, intuitively, what we have to come at by this more roundabout route. They would have felt the shock, the sense of a whole little world being turned upside down, when Jesus of Nazareth, who was going around announcing that God was at last becoming King, looked right inside Levi, Alphie's son, and said 'Follow me!'

In Matthew's gospel this story is part of a string of stories, most of which are healing miracles. There's a good reason for that: this story, too, is a healing miracle. When Jesus goes off to dinner in Levi's house, and the self-appointed guardians of tradition grumble (because if you're announcing the kingdom of God you don't associate with people like that), Jesus replies with a medical metaphor. Those who are well don't need the doctor; it's those who are ill who need the doctor. It's a healing miracle, all right. Levi, Alphie's son, was never the same again. Somebody had treated him as a human being. Somebody had *wanted* him. Did he even dare recognize that somebody had *loved* him? True healing begins in the heart, and I reckon that's

where Jesus' words and action touched and found Levi,
Alphie's boy.

In Mark's gospel, this story is part of his build-up of
showing that the work of Jesus is bringing into being God's
whole new order, his new world. It's the new wine that is
going to burst the old bottles. Now that the sun has risen,
you can blow out the candles. Now that Jesus is here,
everything is to be stood on its head. That's what Mark is
saying. But the new way, the Jesus revolution, isn't just
novelty for novelty's sake. It was the new thing for which
Israel had been longing. And she'd been longing for it for
at least eight centuries, ever since the prophet Hosea
penned these haunting words (14.1–4):

> Israel, come back to the Lord your God;
> your iniquity was the cause of your downfall.
> Provide yourself with words
> and come back to the Lord.
> Say to him, 'Take all iniquity away
> so that we may have happiness again
> and offer you our words of praise . . .'
> I will heal their disloyalty,
> I will love them with all my heart,
> for my anger has turned from them.

This is a prophecy of God restoring Israel; and of Israel
recognizing that her sins have caused her ruin, and turning
back to the God who still loves her freely and faithfully.
Now ask yourself: what would that prophecy look like if it
were to clothe itself in flesh and blood? Might it not look
like a young man going around Galilee making all things
new by loving the unlovable, by healing the unhealable, by
welcoming the outcasts? It's not the healthy who need a
doctor, but the sick; I didn't come to call the righteous, but
sinners. That's the great joke of the gospel. The minute you

think you're good enough for God, God says, 'I'm not interested in people who are good enough for me.' And the minute you think you're too bad for God, God says, 'It's you I've come for.'

There are two things which come bubbling out of this happy and subversive little story which I think we should grasp. The first is obvious and well known and central. (I sometimes worry about insulting people's intelligence by telling them things they already know very well; but, just as I don't get tired of hearing Schubert's Mass in G and Mozart's *Ave Verum* on a regular basis, and indeed would grumble if I didn't, so I hope we don't get tired of hearing what is, to me, the theological equivalent, and indeed the theological basis, of those two astonishing pieces.) When we come to worship, and to the Eucharist in particular, we come into the presence of Almighty God, and to feast at his table, not because we are good people, but because we are forgiven sinners. We come, as we come to a doctor, not because we are well but because we are sick. We come, not because we've got it all together, but because God's got it all together and has invited us to join him. We come, not because our hands are full of our own self-importance or self-righteousness, but because they are empty and waiting to receive his love, his body and blood, his own very self.

This is as basic to Christianity as the ball is to football. And, just as you have a rotten game of football if people ignore the ball and simply tackle the opposition, or even the crowd, so you have a pretty poor time in church if you forget for a moment that we are here because we don't deserve to be. And when that truth gets hold of you, and sinks down inside you like a hot drink on a cold day, then the effect on the whole life of the Christian community is quite marvellous. We are all here by grace alone: so we can relax. You don't have anything to *prove* in the presence of God; you shouldn't have anything to prove, either, in the presence of your fellow Christians. You don't have to pretend in the presence of God; no more should you need to pretend in the presence of your fellow Christians. The ground is level at the foot of the cross; the only people who are excluded from the party are those who exclude themselves, by supposing they don't need the cross, don't need God's forgiveness, don't need the free love of Jesus, in the first place.

So the first thing that comes at me out of the story of Levi, son of Alphaeus, is the simple basic truth that God in Christ loves and accepts us as we are, and invites us into fellowship with him, and with each other, on the basis of that love rather than anything in ourselves:

> Love bade me welcome: yet my soul drew back,
>   Guiltie of dust and sinne.
> But quick-ey'd Love, observing me grow slack
>   From my first entrance in,
> Drew nearer to me, sweetly questioning
>   If I lack'd any thing.
>
> A guest, I answer'd, worthy to be here':
>   Love said, 'You shall be he.'
> 'I, the unkind, ungrateful? Ah, my dear,
>   I cannot look on Thee.
> Love took my hand, and smiling did reply,
>   'Who made the eyes but I?'
>
> 'Truth, Lord; but I have marr'd them; let my shame
>   Go where it doth deserve.'
> 'And know you not,' says Love, 'Who bore the blame?'
>   'My dear, then I will serve.'
> 'You must sit down,' says Love, 'and taste my meat.'
>   So I did sit and eat.

(George Herbert, 'Love')

The other point that comes out of this story to me forms a direct challenge to the contemporary church. Think back to Hosea's prophecy for a moment. 'I will heal their disloyalty, I will love them with all my heart, for my anger has turned from them.' What would that prophecy look like if it were to become flesh and blood *today*? Answer that question, and we have written ourselves an agenda for mission. 'It isn't the healthy that need a doctor, but the sick.' What sort of things might the church be doing if we needed to explain them with an aphorism like that? If we aren't doing anything that needs that sort of explanation, then we need to ask ourselves whether we are in fact presenting the gospel of Jesus Christ to today's world. We must be ready to challenge society in Jesus' name. Jesus himself, after all, challenged his own society by overturning its expectations, and celebrating the kingdom of God with, as it seemed, all the wrong people.

What matters, as we consider our mission and how to go about it, is that we should be considering where the real need is in our society, and how we can meet that need. This is partly, of course, to do with money. When, as a church community, not least in a cathedral, we raise money, part of what we pledge goes of course to important charitable causes elsewhere. Part of what we spend on the cathedral itself goes precisely to make it place a place of welcome, of love, of gospel for all who come. One of the reasons I dislike the idea of cathedrals balancing their books by charging tourists for admission is that I believe we should present to our visitors the welcome of Jesus, not the outstretched hand of Levi, Alphie's son. But if we are to manage that, and so enable such buildings to exercise their unique mission (English cathedrals see more of the unchurched population than all other 'religious' buildings in the country put together), those who regularly use them (whether their regular congregation, their local community, or their diocese) need to be supporting their gospel mission from their own resources and initiatives as far as they can.

But, though money is important, it's not all-important. Everybody gave Levi money; Jesus gave him something else. He gave him back his humanity. We need to look around us and discover where people are being dehumanized – by their jobs or their lack of jobs, by their homes or their lack of homes, by their families or their lack of families. We need to find ways of communicating to them what Jesus communicated to Levi ben Alphaeus: that they are human beings, that they are valuable, that they don't need to prove anything, that they don't need to pretend. We need to communicate to them that God loves them.

A well-designed church or cathedral is put together in order to say that, but we need to be sure that it does. Most churches could do more than they do through exhibitions and displays; but the human welcome that people receive is far and away the most important thing. Church music is designed to express the richness and wonder of God's love, and church musicians need to be supported in giving us this priceless gift day by day and week by week. But these are only a beginning. There are many other ways of telling people that God loves them. There are projects for the homeless, for those below the poverty line. There are people in prison who need visiting. There are hospitals and hospices that depend very considerably on volunteer help. And so on. This usually means doing things more than saying things. Remember what St Francis said to his friars as he sent them out: 'Preach the gospel of Jesus by every means possible; and, if it's really necessary, you could even use words.'

And it all comes down to the little command which Jesus gave to Levi, Alphie's son, that strange day in Capernaum. The one thing people didn't want Levi to do was to follow them. They wanted to leave him behind, to forget about him, to put him out of their minds, to concentrate on the nice people, the lovable people, not those who made them angry, or ashamed, or afraid. And Jesus said, 'Follow me.' Follow me, Levi ben Alphaeus; follow me to the party, where the love of God flows like new wine and everyone can drink as much of it as they want; follow me to the table where we all look into one another's eyes without pretending and without needing to prove anything. But, Levi, this party isn't just for you. Once the doctor has cured you, you must in your turn become a doctor. Follow me to where people are feeling like you used to feel. Follow me to the people with hard faces and with sad faces, with hard hearts and with bitter hearts. Follow me to the rich people who are afraid of the poor, and to the poor people who are jealous of the rich. Follow me to the people who weep every day, and to the people who have forgotten how to weep. Follow me, and do as I do, love as I love.

Jesus didn't ask much of Levi ben Alphaeus. He asked everything, because he had just given everything. And Levi, perhaps to his own and certainly to the onlookers' astonishment, got up and followed him.

He was only doing what he was told.

CHAPTER TEN

Bethany

Come with me to Bethany. It's not far to go, if you're in Jerusalem; but it's quite a steep walk. If you came this way, taking the route you would be likely to take, from the place you would be likely to come from, you would go down: down into the Kidron valley, across the brook, and past the garden of Gethsemane; then up, steeply up, further up than you'd gone down before, until you would stand at last, out of breath, on the summit of the Mount of Olives, looking back at Jerusalem the golden. It's only a mile or so, but it's quite a climb. That was the route taken at night by the broken king, David, when Absalom rebelled. It was the route travelled by Jesus and his disciples, night after night during Holy Week, until, for reasons Jesus knew but they did not, they remained on the last night down in Gethsemane, and waited. And, night after night, from the crest of the Mount of Olives they would go on just a short way more, inside another mile, and would arrive at Bethany.

And there they went on that last day, the day Luke describes at the end of his gospel. 'Then he took them out as far as Bethany, and lifting up his hands he blessed them. Now as he blessed them, he withdrew from them and was carried up to heaven.' And let's not be fooled, while we're on the subject, by the naive literalism of certain paintings of the ascension, and for that matter certain hymns, which speak of Jesus going 'to his home above the skies', as though Jesus were some kind of primitive space-traveller. Heaven, as I have said elsewhere, is not a place thousands of miles up, or for that matter down, in our space, nor would it help us if it were. It is God's dimension of ordinary reality, the dimension which is normally hidden but which we penetrate mysteriously, or rather which penetrates us mysteriously, in prayer, in the scriptures, in the breaking of the bread. So when you stand on the outskirts of Bethany, and think of Jesus' withdrawal from the disciples, you are not here to verify, instruct yourself, inform curiosity or carry report. You are here to kneel where prayer has been valid.

And prayer is indeed valid here, on the Mount of Ascension, because Jesus' ascension is the great symbol of prayer. It isn't just that the ascended Lord is constantly interceding for his people before the Father's throne, true though that is. It is, more, that his ascension sums up what prayer actually is. A human being goes through the thin veil into the very presence of God, there to be welcomed, to worship, to love, to intercede. As so often in Christian theology, the best definition is not an abstract formula but a human being, indeed *the* human being, Jesus. That is why we pray *to* the Father *through* Jesus the Son. He is, quite literally, the Way. That is what the ascension is all about. And the journey to this point is always short, but steep.

So let's allow Bethany to stand for the rest of the gospel story, and ask again who it is that is the Way, who it is that is now enthroned as Lord of the world. What else happened at Bethany? Well, that's where Jesus got the donkey, for a start. No doubt there is much we could learn from that, but I want to choose three other Bethany incidents, three little vignettes which put some flesh and blood on the otherwise somewhat abstract doctrine of the ascension. When we think of the ascended Lord as the Bethany Jesus, what picture do we get?

Bethany was, first, the home of Mary and Martha. Think back to Luke chapter 10, the well-known Mary-and-Martha story. Jesus is visiting the sisters, and precipitates a domestic crisis. What's the problem? We normally regard Mary and Martha simply as typical of the passive and the active personalities, or, in Christian terms, of the life of devotion on the one hand and the life of service on the other. That may well be one level of the story, but it isn't the whole truth. The problem is not simply that Mary is so starry-eyed, listening to Jesus, that she forgets to help with the washing-up. The problem is that in that culture men and women belong in different parts of the building, and Mary has shamelessly gone across the short but steep gulf that separates male and female space.

What's more, she has assumed the posture of a disciple, a learner. She is sitting at Jesus' feet; which is the equivalent, in that culture, to somebody sitting at a desk in a classroom in modern Western life. You sit at the feet of a rabbi, like Saul of Tarsus sitting at the feet of Gamaliel, in order that one day you may be a rabbi yourself.

So Martha's excuse about the washing-up looks like a coded way of saying: 'stop this shameless behaviour and leave our social world intact.' She is telling Jesus to reproach Mary, but actually she is reproaching Jesus too. And Jesus, there in Bethany, declares that Mary has chosen the better part. Jesus quietly and calmly dismantles a major social taboo and leaves the onlookers open-mouthed in amazement. This is the Bethany Jesus; should we be surprised to find that the Lord of the world has the right to turn the world upside down?

And not only the world, but life and death themselves. Come back to Bethany some time later, and find the same two sisters in the very depth of shock and grief. 'Lord, if you had been here, my brother would not have died.' They both say it, with the reproach of grief: Lord, we needed

you and you weren't here! (Have you ever said that?) And
the Bethany Jesus, the one we know as the ascended Lord,
finds his own grief welling up in sympathy with these dear
sisters, and we have that awesome little verse in John
11.35: 'Jesus wept.' And, still greatly distressed, he comes
to the tomb of Lazarus, and tells them to take away the
stone.

Martha objects – she's always telling Jesus off, bless
her, and he is so gentle with her – Lord, there'll be a smell!
He's been dead four days! But they remove the stone
anyway. Jesus prays a prayer, not of intercession but of
thanksgiving, presumably *because there isn't a smell*; he
has already prayed, and knows he has been heard. And then
he shouts, 'Lazarus; come out!' And Lazarus makes the
short but steep journey from death to life. We die with the
dying: see, they depart, and we go with them. We are born
with the dead: see, they return, and bring us with them.
This is the Bethany Jesus; this is the ascended Lord: the one
who has identified totally with the pain of the world, the
one who has total authority over life and death, and the one
who now prays to the Father for his grief-stricken people.
The ascended Lord is the one who disturbs the comfortable
and comforts the disturbed.

And then another scene we all know very well. Jesus is
again in Bethany, sitting at table, and a woman comes with
a costly jar of ointment, and anoints Jesus with it. Matthew
and Mark tell the story, but don't tell us who it was; John
reveals that this, too, was Mary of Bethany. Well, she
would, wouldn't she? (This probably isn't the same story as
the one in Luke, where a woman who is a sinner comes and
anoints Jesus and is assured of forgiveness. But the point is
not far off.) Mary has discovered that Jesus is worth everything she's got: she has attained that condition of complete
simplicity, costing not less than everything. She has made
the short but steep journey from being around Jesus to

being totally devoted to him. She is worshipping him for all he's worth.

And, as always, when people are worshipping Jesus with everything they've got, some other people find this distasteful and disturbing. This time the coded message comes in terms of money, always a powerful argument for maintaining the *status quo* and the stiff upper lip. It needs to be heard as blustering, embarrassed self-importance: 'This ointment – this ointment – this ointment could have been sold for hundreds of pounds and – and – and given to the poor!' Mary's uninhibited worship has shown up the onlookers' cold formality, has knocked at the door of deep emotion that they had carefully locked up. People resent the Bethany Jesus; they resent, too, the way other people react to him.

We find this blustering self-importance today when people criticize the church for spending money on new silver vessels or on fabulous music. We find it when people lose their inhibitions and want to raise their arms in the air and sing in tongues, or when they want to swing incense around so that the building, like the house in Bethany, is filled with the lovely smell. I suspect we all reach a point where somebody else's enthusiasm strikes us as over the top. But, let's face it, the whole point of enthusiasm is that it's over the top; and if you're not enthusiastic about Jesus, or are tempted to mock at somebody who is, look around within this story and see what company you're keeping.

This, then, is the Bethany Jesus, part three: the Jesus who, on his way to the cross, is worthy of such total and costly devotion that those who don't understand will regard it as crazy. When the ascended Lord comforts the disturbed and disturbs the comforted, the result is reckless adoration. That's what Ascensiontide is all about.

Where have we got to so far, following this Bethany Jesus, this ascended Lord? He is the Lord who turns the world upside down. He is the one who sympathizes totally with us in our sadness, our failure, our grief. He is the one whose prayer to the Father brings life out of death. And he is the one who deserves our most costly devotion. Let Bethany stand for all the other incidents in the gospels, and this is the story of Jesus in miniature. These are, of course, some of the traditional themes of Ascensiontide: Jesus the ruler of the world, Jesus the great high priest, Jesus ever living to make intercession for us, Jesus the object of our love and worship. But there is one more, which Luke would not have us forget. And to find it I want to take you once more on that short but steep journey.

Some years ago, at Ascensiontide, I was in Jerusalem, teaching at the Hebrew University. I used to walk out of the old city, across the head of the Kidron valley, and up to the campus on Mount Scopus, just to the north of the Mount of Olives. And one afternoon, as I was half-way through my lecture, we heard three muffled but quite loud explosions.

Now in Israel you often hear odd noises. Sometimes it's military planes breaking the sound barrier; it's such a small country, so they have to train over built-up areas. Sometimes it's fireworks, when someone's having a party. Sometimes it's gunfire. These explosions weren't quite like any of those. We looked at one another, shrugged our shoulders, and I went on with the lecture (which, ironically enough, was on Romans 9—11, Paul's classic statement about God's struggle with Israel). It was only that night, on the television news, that I discovered what had happened. The Israeli army had caught three teenage Arab boys who, as part of their regular protest against the occupation of their territories, had been throwing stones at the soldiers. The army did what they usually did. They went to the boys' homes. They ordered everybody out. They packed the three houses with explosives. And they blew them up. Three sad, squat piles of rubble, containing the thousand little things that make a house a home. And the village where this took place, on that bright, sunny afternoon, was of course Bethany. (And do you know, when I told my Israeli friends what I thought of this barbaric behaviour, they told me with a wry smile that it was a trick they had learned from the British in the 1940s.)

And I wanted to say – Lord, if only you had been there! Lord, if you're the Lord of the world, why are people still blowing up each other's houses? Lord, isn't it time for this barbaric behaviour to be broken through just like you broke through the old taboos? And Bethany, of course, stands once more for the whole story: for Bosnia, for Rwanda, for Ireland, for Somalia, for Central America, the litany that becomes so familiar that the pain is dulled and we shrug our shoulders and walk away. And I go back to Luke's story of the ascension, and I find the answer staring me in the face.

One of the last things that Jesus said to his followers before they went on that short and steep journey to Bethany was this: that, in his name, 'repentance and forgiveness of sins should be preached to all the nations, beginning from Jerusalem' (Luke 24.47).

Now, listen: we have trivialized that message. We have reduced it in scale; we have brought it down to our level to make it bearable. We have thought that it meant simply that I should repent of my sins, and you of yours, and that God would forgive us. And of course it does mean that, and without that there is no personal gospel; but it means much, much more. What is the announcement that the church must make to the world? It isn't simply that every individual is a sinner and needs to repent, true though that is. It is that the way the world lives is out of joint with the way that God intends; and that God in Christ is holding out a different way to live, a way which is characterized, at every level, by forgiveness. When people glimpse the forgiveness of God in Christ, they are set free from the need to clutch at their own security and to blow up those who threaten them, even when they're boys throwing stones. Forgiveness is the most powerful thing in the world, because it is the gift of the ascended Lord not only to his church but also to his bombed-out world.

Think how it works. The world, like Martha, says: 'We must do things this way; this is the only way we know how to live.' No, says the Bethany Jesus, there is a different way to live, which will turn your world upside down. The world, like Martha and Mary, stands weeping at the tomb, saying there's no point opening this all up because it'll only stink. No, says the Bethany Jesus; I have prayed to the Father, and there is life hidden in that tomb. The world, like Judas, stands mocking at those who worship Jesus with everything they've got; what use will that be in addressing the problems of society? Every use possible, says the Bethany Jesus: it has been written that the Messiah should suffer and rise again, and that, as Lord of the world, he should send out his heralds to announce to the world that there is a different way of living, a different way of being human, a way characterized by forgiveness through and through.

This is what it means for the ascended Lord to entrust his church with the task of evangelism. Evangelism is not simply a matter of bringing individuals to personal faith, though of course that remains central to the whole enterprise. It is a matter of confronting the world with the good, but deeply disturbing, news of a different way of living, which is the Bethany way, the way of love. With the drawing of this Love and the voice of this Calling, we shall not cease from exploration, and the end of all our exploring will be to arrive where we started and know the place for the first time.

The Bethany Jesus comforts the disturbed and disturbs the comfortable. He wants us to be his agents in doing so. For this, we need to know that he is the ascended Lord of the world; and we need to be indwelt by his Spirit. The life of heaven, through the prayer of the ascended Lord, is to become the life of earth.

Come with me, then, to Bethany. It's a short journey, but a steep one. From here, on a clear day, you can see for ever.

CHAPTER ELEVEN

When I am Weak

Nearly twenty years ago I found myself at a large conference, and I bumped into a man I vaguely knew. He had just been appointed as principal of a small seminary in the United States. He was looking for some new junior faculty members, and asked me if I was interested. I suppose I must have given him some encouragement, because his next question was: 'Do you have a copy of your *curriculum vitae*?'

I was astonished. He seemed to think that the average person, or at least the average academic, would naturally be walking around with a *curriculum vitae* handy on the off-chance that someone might want to see it. This struck me then, and strikes me still, as faintly absurd. It makes sense only in a society where too many people take themselves too seriously. I sometimes think that every time one has to make up a *curriculum vitae*, for a job or whatever, one ought at the same time to make up, at least for one's own benefit, an inverted list: the exams I didn't pass, the jobs I didn't get, the short story no one would publish.

For America, read Corinth; for the inverted *curriculum vitae*, read 2 Corinthians 11 and 12. To get the flavour, imagine me presenting to my over-solemn acquaintance that upside-down list of all my failures and disappointments. You see, the Corinthian church had started to take themselves too seriously. Now that they'd been Christians for a little while they wanted to go up-market. They'd had some new teachers in town, who had given them the idea that they could aspire to higher standards of wisdom, to higher levels of spiritual attainment, to more dramatic experiences, to greater triumphs for the gospel. This was very exciting; it was also very beguiling. Instead of being regarded as the lowest of the low, as a little group of crazy fanatics that had dropped off the bottom of the social ladder, maybe this new teaching, this new wisdom, might actually advance their social standing just a bit. Maybe, with these new teachers, their church would be famous, looked up to . . .

And where did that leave Paul? Well, Paul had been their own evangelist and founder, they couldn't deny that. But, in the light of all that they'd heard from these new teachers, they were tempted to look at Paul in the way that young people, spending a week in the big city, may be tempted to think of the folks back home: a bit boring, a bit shabby – just a bit dull. And the new teachers seem to have suggested that actually Paul was more interested in his other churches anyway; after all, it was a long time since he'd been to see them . . .

Paul was clearly hurt by this nonsense, but he was far more worried at the sheer pride – social pride and spiritual pride – that he detected in Corinth. And what the Corinthians didn't know was that he had just come through something like a total nervous breakdown, and in any case had only just got out of prison in Ephesus, so he wasn't in great shape to sail straight over and sort them out face to face. So he travelled round the north end of the Aegean, and as he travelled he thought and prayed and worried. And then at a certain point I think I see a slow smile coming across his face, as he starts to plan the letter he will write to them.

He has some specific things to say anyway. He is collecting money on behalf of the poverty-stricken Christians in Judaea, and he wants to make sure the Corinthians have got enough laid by to put up a decent sum. But the bulk of the letter is an explanation of what being an apostle really means. All right, he says. You want my *curriculum vitae*. You want my up-to-date testimony. You want my full credentials as an apostle. You want to know all the wonderful things I have done for God, all the battles I have fought and the victories I have won in the service of the kingdom, all the things that will enable you to hold your heads high in front of your pagan neighbours. Very well, get a load of this. I am the most superior apostle imaginable – because I'm a habitual jailbird; I've lost count of my beatings; I've been through humiliating punishments, I've been stoned, three times I've been shipwrecked, I've been constantly in danger, and I'm always anxious about all the churches. Paul's *curriculum vitae* is upside-down. He's boasting of all the wrong things. They want his successes, not his failures. They want his triumphs, not his disasters. They want him to play the hero, and he plays the fool.

But they are the real fools. They have exchanged the gospel of the crucified Messiah for the gospel of success; and the only way Paul can get through to them is through this shameless tease, exposing their pride for what it is. And this brings us to 2 Corinthians 12. They want his up-to-date spiritual testimony, do they? They want to know what splendid visions and revelations he has been experiencing, do they? They want an account of his great supernatural power, do they? Fine, here we go. I know a man in Christ – he won't even say it's himself to begin with – who *fourteen years ago* [come on, Paul, we want something more up-to-date than that!] was caught up into the third heaven, and – well, actually, I don't know much about what was going on, he says, and I'm not allowed to tell you what I heard. Yes, it was wonderful, but that's about it. (It reminds me of when Einstein was asked when he normally had his original ideas. He replied that actually he hadn't had that many.)

And then Paul comes to the crunch. 'To keep me from being too elated, I was given a thorn in the flesh.' He won't even say what it was, but it was clearly an unpleasant affliction. 'Three times', he says, 'I prayed to the Lord about this, that it would leave me' [yes, yes, think the Corinthians, now we're getting there – a great healing miracle coming up] – 'but he said to me, "My grace is sufficient for you; power is perfected in weakness." So where does this leave me? I will boast gladly of my weaknesses, so that Christ's power may dwell in me. I am content with weaknesses, insults, hardships, persecutions, and calamities for Christ's sake; for when I am weak, then I am strong.'

I like to imagine the scene in the Christian assembly in Corinth as this letter is read out. There they are, fifty or sixty of them perhaps, crammed into the house of one of the few wealthy Christians in the town. They have just watched their new ideas dismantled from behind with breath-taking skill by the one they regarded as a bit old hat, a bit dull. But the whole point of what he's been saying is that skill and strength and pride and power aren't where it's at. Do we follow a crucified Messiah, or do we follow some happy hero-figure?

And do you see what Paul has achieved, in fact, through this letter, through this astonishing irony and teasing? We often think of Jesus Christ as the great healer, but this passage sounds as though it should be entitled 'When Christ Refused to Heal.' But what Paul has done is in fact to effect a healing miracle at a much deeper level. Who cares whether the thorn remains in the flesh or not, if the body of Christ is deeply sick with spiritual pride? Who cares about private visions and revelations if the community of the people of God cares more for status and prestige than for the shameful gospel of the cross?

What was their disease? The Corinthians had not, perhaps, gone very far down the road along which their new teachers had enticed them. A mile or two further on, they would have prided themselves on being *Corinthian* Christians, rather than those backward heretical Philippians or Ephesians. A little way beyond that, they would have become syncretistic, picking up every new spiritual experience they could find, whether it had anything to do with Jesus and the cross or not. And before very long they would have set up on their own; or rather, they would have broken up into different groups, because once you contract the Corinthian disease you become vulnerable to personality cults (disguised, of course, as doctrinal or ethical debates); or perhaps to battles between different cultural styles in worship (disguised, of course, as the distinction between the truly spiritual and the merely aesthetic).

And what is the remedy? It's no good Paul giving them a lecture, bullying them or harrying them into line. Silly old Paul, they'll say; we're bored with you. Nor will it simply do for him to back off, to sit and sulk, or perhaps pray, in Ephesus or wherever. The love of Christ, as he says in 2 Corinthians 5, leaves him no choice. He must come to the place where they are; he is on his way, physically, but in this letter he is coming to meet them emotionally and spiritually and deeply personally. He is coming, out of his own pain, both emotional and physical, to apply his own love, his own upside-down wisdom, his own humour and irony, his own knowledge of Christ, to the place where the disease has got hold of them. He stands in the middle, holding fast to Christ with one hand, and holding fast to them with the other, even though it stretches him into the agonizing but familiar position that suggests the healing is starting to work. This, as we saw in chapter 6 of the present book, is what he means when he talks about the ministry of reconciliation.

How would you like to be Paul? Not a lot, I should think. Shipwreck, beating, worry, danger, prison: forget it.

But it's not so good not being Paul either, when you think about it. How do you cope when the world is out of joint? When *your* world is out of joint? When people you love are at odds with one another or with you? When you can see people, perhaps people you care for very deeply, going off in the wrong direction while claiming that it's you that's heading the wrong way? The temptation is either to yell at people, or to back off and sulk in a corner. That's the way of not being Paul; it's not very effective, and it's not much fun.

But what does it mean to be Paul in such situations? It means thinking right into the problem and the pain of the situation you face, even if that means allowing some of your own raw nerves, some of your own vulnerability, to be exposed. It means being weak in order to be strong. We live in a world full of people struggling to be, or at least to appear, strong, in order not to be weak; and we follow a gospel which says that when I am weak, then I am strong. And this gospel is the only thing that brings true healing.

The calling to imitate Paul is obviously the calling to imitate Christ. From the whole way we have come at it, this is obviously the call to be Christ's agents in working healing miracles: not necessarily in healing physical ailments, though that can and does happen today (never predictably, always humblingly), but also in healing personal, emotional, psychological, social, cultural wounds and scars. Please note, if Paul is anything to go by (and he is), you don't have to be healthy to be a healer. It is the wounded surgeon who plies the steel most successfully; 'beneath the bleeding hands we feel the sharp compassion of the healer's art.'

What is our calling, then? We are called, simply, to hold on to Christ and his cross with one hand, with all our might; and to hold on to those we are given to love with the other hand, with all our might, with courage, humour, self-abandonment, creativity, flair, tears, silence, sympathy, gentleness, flexibility, Christlikeness. When we find their tears becoming our own, we may know that healing has begun to happen; when they find Christ in being held on to by us, whether we realize it or not, we are proving the truth of what Paul said: God made him to be sin for us, who knew no sin, so that in him we might embody the saving faithfulness of God.

This calling comes in at least three varieties, or levels. We are all called to the first; and such insight as we gain from that will help those who aren't called to the second and third to pray intelligently, at least, for those who are.

The first level of calling, in many ways the most important, comes to all human beings, men, women and children in Christ. Wherever you are, whoever you are with, you are called – we are all called – to hold on to Christ firmly with one hand and to hold on to those around with the other, in prayer, discussion, generosity, gratitude, teaching or learning, caring or being cared for. You will never meet anybody, and you will never meet any group of people, that does not need healing in some respect or other; and God will see to it, whether you realize it or not, that their pain and yours are often remarkably similar, so that all you may have to do, to share the work of Christ the healer, is to hold on and pray in silent sympathy. There will be other times when the work of healing will require all your resources of courage, to confront and challenge folly and wickedness, but to do it as one who knows their power and allure. There will be times when healing will come through humour, through cooking, through play. Paul had to call on all his rhetorical skill, not in order to teach but in order to heal. Whatever skills God has given you, be prepared to use them as instruments of the gospel.

But the second level of calling, which may, and I pray will, come to some of you, is the calling to be all this for the church. It is the call, in other words, to full-time Christian ministry at whatever level, including that of ordination. Ordination isn't the be-all and end-all of Christian ministry; but the church desperately needs ordained clergy, needs them now as much as ever, and I would be surprised if out of the readers of a book like this God were not calling someone, perhaps several, to give their life in imitation of Paul in imitation of Christ: to hold on to Christ with one hand and hold on to the church with the other, to share and feel the agony of the church's follies and failings, and to know the power of Christ to restore and heal the church and set her feet back on the right path. That is a vocation not to be lightly dismissed.

The church, after all, needs leaders who can break new ground for others to follow. The church needs teachers who can expound the scriptures and find fresh ways of presenting the story of God's love. But, above all, the church needs healers who can be channels of God's peace and love, who can be for her today what Paul was for Corinth, a wise and faithful friend who wounds in order to heal, who tells the truth not to hurt but to mend, who rejoices with the joyful and weeps with the mourners, who teases and plays, who agonizes and prays, who shares the priestly and healing work of Christ. The church doesn't need people who know it all, or can do it all, or want to control it all. When I am weak, then I am strong.

The third level of calling ought to be in our prayers especially at times of crisis, such as we face in many parts of the Western world at the moment. There is a desperate need for people to do for the world, for society as a whole and in its various parts, what Paul did for Corinth.

Our hearts go out to those who suffer through terrorist action, through war and civil conflict, and through the countless waking nightmares that we see and hear in the news media day by day. And what is needed, in so many areas of national life as well, such as prisons, health services, schools and colleges, inner cities, racial minorities, the unemployed, and of course politics itself – what is needed all over our society is the one thing the Thatcherite and Reaganite revolution forgot to cater for: healers.

Why healers? We don't need people to yell at these situations or to bully them. We don't need people to back off and pretend it's somebody else's problem. We need Christian people to work as healers: as healing judges and prison staff, as healing teachers and administrators, as healing shopkeepers and bankers, as healing musicians and artists, as healing writers and scientists, as healing diplomats and politicians. We need people who will hold on to Christ firmly with one hand and reach out the other, with wit and skill and cheerfulness, with compassion and sorrow and tenderness, to the places where our world is in pain. We need people who will use all their god-given skills, as Paul used his, to analyse where things have gone wrong, to come to the place of pain, and to hold over the wound the only medicine which will really heal, which is the love of Christ made incarnate once more, the strange love of God turned into your flesh and mine, your smile and mine, your tears and mine, your patient analysis and mine, your frustration and mine, your joy and mine.

This isn't a matter of having all the answers or taking control of the world. Indeed, it's just the opposite. When I am weak, then I am strong. We must pray for the Middle East; for the countries of the former Soviet bloc; for Northern Ireland; and for so many other situations we could name around the world. We must pray that God will raise up a new generation of strong weaklings; of wise fools; of wounded healers; so that the healing love of Christ may flow out into the world, to confront violence and injustice with the rebuke of the cross, and to comfort the injured and wronged with the consolation of the cross.

Somebody said on the television recently, concerning Northern Ireland, that it would take a miracle to sort things out now. Yes, indeed, and that, once again, is what Jesus specializes in; but miracles come in all shapes and sizes. 'My grace is sufficient for you, for power is made perfect in weakness.' Please God there may not be lacking men, women and children of holy courage in Northern Ireland, in Bosnia, in the Middle East, and elsewhere, who will be that miracle in their lives, their love, their hope and their faith. And please God may we, in whatever vocation he calls us, be that same miracle there. For when we are weak, then we are strong.

CHAPTER TWELVE

Getting Back on the Road

The newspapers always like a good religious story. Actually, what they like is a good religious *controversy*; a scandal, an argument, another variation on the old 'trads v. rads' theme. But there's one theme that they don't touch these days. Even during the Week of Prayer for Christian Unity, they never seem to talk about the quest for church unity, the ecumenical movement.

Well, they wouldn't, would they? The ecumenical movement is no longer news. The heady days of the sixties and seventies, when for a while it looked as though major steps towards visible union were going to come about, have passed. Ecumenical projects have come and gone. Many ordinary Christians in the Western world have become accustomed to praying for the unity of all Christian people in the way that many pray for the eventual coming of the kingdom – something greatly to be desired, no doubt, but it doesn't seem to affect particularly what we actually do from week to week.

I believe it is time to get things back on track. If we worship the one true and living God, how can we not grieve over disunity in the church? If we worship the God of love revealed in Jesus, how can we not long for the loving unity of all those who respond to that love? If we worship the God revealed in the life-giving Spirit, why shouldn't we invoke that Spirit to bring us together?

To this end, I'm going to look at one of the great Pauline passages that speaks of the unity of the church, namely, a quite remarkable text in Galatians chapter 2. Here is Paul, talking about himself, but even more about someone else:

> I have been crucified with Christ; and it is no longer I who live, but Christ who lives in me. And the life I now live in the flesh I live by faith in the Son of God, who loved me and gave himself for me. (Galatians 2.19–20)

You might suppose that this is simply a rather lavish way of describing Paul's conversion and its permanent consequences. What had happened to him could only be described as dying and coming back to life – or rather, going on through death and out into a new sort of life. In recognizing that the crucified Jesus was the Messiah, Paul came to see that he, as a zealous Jew, had to regard himself as completely identified with, and loyal to, this Messiah. And that meant that he, Saul of Tarsus, had in one sense to lose his identity completely, in order to find a new identity as 'a man in Christ'.

But what has that, in turn, got to do with Paul's vision for the unity of the church? Well, from Paul's point of view, everything. Paul isn't just indulging in a bit of autobiography for its own sake. This description of his dying and rising with Christ is the climax of a long paragraph, in which Paul tells of the confrontation he had had with Peter in Antioch. And that confrontation was all about the unity of the church.

Let's back up a bit and consider what was at stake. Galatians 2 is all about the question: who are Christians allowed to eat with? This was a major issue for the early church. Paul's response remains enormously important.

Paul's altercation with Peter arose like this. Peter had been visiting the church in Antioch (Paul's home church), where Jewish and Gentile Christians used to eat together perfectly happily; and Peter had joined in without scruple. Until, that is, certain persons came from James, in Jerusalem; whereupon Peter separated himself and ate only with other Jews, presumably Jewish Christians. Who was right? Peter or Paul?

Paul addressed the question in terms of the doctrine we have come to call 'justification by faith', ending with the remarkable passage I quoted a moment ago. Justification, of course, has been for four hundred years one of the main sticking points in discussions between Protestants and Catholics. Paul's point, however, is this: if you understand justification by faith, you will be left in no doubt about who you may sit down and eat with. The whole discussion is about *community definition*. The thrust of it all for us today, I believe, is that the original Pauline doctrine of justification *is not only something that all Christians might be able to agree on, but, ironically, that it is in itself the original and the strongest ecumenical doctrine.* It isn't just that if we really try hard in our doctrinal discussions we might come up with a formula which enables us to bury the hatchet from centuries of acrimonious debate about justification; justification is itself the doctrine that tells us *that* we *should* bury the hatchet and, moreover, tells us *how* we might do it.

You see, Saul of Tarsus and his pre-Christian Jewish friends didn't just sit around discussing religious doctrines. They were eager for Israel's God to act, to bring in his kingdom; and this would consist, they believed, of the victory of God over the pagan, Gentile nations. All their praying and their politicking were bent to this end. And, as zealous Jews to this day believe, the only way this would happen was if Israel stopped flirting with paganism and maintained herself as the holy people of God, true to the law, separate from the rest of the world. Saul of Tarsus had been longing for a national and ethnic liberation in which Israel would become, publicly and visibly, the true people of the one true God.

So, in the church in Antioch, within a very few years of Pentecost, Peter found himself caught in the cross-fire between two clearly thought out positions.

The Jerusalem Christians were quite clear. They were Jewish Christians; and because of their zeal for God, and their hostility to Gentiles, they were unwilling to share fellowship with Gentile Christians unless they became circumcised. The hope of ethnic Israel was still paramount. From their point of view, failure to get circumcised represented a lack of seriousness about the Gentiles' commitment to the God of Abraham, Isaac and Jacob.

Paul's position was equally clear, and far more radical. The renewed people of God in Christ were a single people, he insisted; they were called, in principle, from every nation under heaven, and did not require any racial or cultural qualification. Their belief in the gospel of Jesus was the only badge of membership. That's what 'justification by faith' was all about.

And poor old Peter is embarrassed. He is caught between the two. And, when he draws back, and decides not to eat with the Gentile Christians any longer, the other Jewish Christians in Antioch withdraw as well, including even Barnabas, Paul's close associate and travelling companion.

Paul, telling the Galatians what he said to Peter, puts his finger on the critical issue (2.14). Peter is a Jew; fine. But Peter, who had believed all along that Jesus was the Messiah, had come to realize that this meant crucifixion and resurrection. Peter had himself pioneered the mission to the Gentiles, accepting freely and without racial constraint those who believed in Jesus. Now, Paul says, by your own action you are saying to your Gentile fellow Christians that they are second-class citizens; if they want to become full members of God's people, they must get circumcised and become adopted into the Jewish people. That, from Paul's point of view, was a contradiction in terms.

So, in addressing Peter, Paul articulates the all-time basis for the unity of all Christian people. Membership in God's family is not by race, but by grace. It is not by moralism, but by the forgiving love of God. It is not tied to a particular culture or class or gender; the ground is level at the foot of the cross. As he sums it up a chapter later, there is neither Jew nor Greek, slave nor free, male nor female; all are one in Christ Jesus.

The only badge of membership, therefore, is that which is the same for us all: the saving act of God in Christ Jesus, and the helpless acceptance of that by the believer, simply in the act of believing itself. That's justification by faith. And that, not just a private spiritual experience, however dramatic, is what Paul is talking about in the passage with which I began (vv. 19–20):

> Through the law I died to the law, so that I might live to God. I have been crucified with Christ; it is no longer I who live, but Christ who lives in me. And the life I now live in the flesh I live by faith in the Son of God, who loved me and gave himself for me.

Paul, not for the last time, is using himself as the example of what happens to the typical Jew when fully faced by the revelation of the living God in the face of the crucified and risen Jesus Christ. He is, quite simply, turned inside out.

Let's go through, step by step, the thrust of what he's saying, not just about himself but about the whole purposes of God. The Messiah represents Israel; the Messiah has died and been raised: so those who recognize him as Messiah discover that God's plan was always cross-shaped; they are co-crucified with the Messiah, and given a new life, the Messianic life, which redefines their identity. They are no longer labelled by their ethnic, territorial or cultural setting, but simply as 'the Messiah's people', people 'in Christ'. Jewish Christians have come out of the defining context of the Jewish law; that is no longer where their identity lies. Gentile Christians have come out of the defining context of their social and cultural worlds. That is no longer where their true identity lies.

Jew and Gentile alike have thus come alive in a new way to the living God. The life they have is not, however, that which their parents bequeathed them, circumscribed by family, land, and tribal taboos. The life all Christians have is defined by faith in, or perhaps by the faithfulness of, the Son of God; and the Son of God is known as 'the one who loved me and gave himself for me'. As so often in Paul, at the heart of the doctrine there is no cold mind, but a warm heart; no abstract system, but the act of love and the response of love.

For Paul, therefore, to step back even for a second into a world where one is defined in terms of race, geography, cultic taboos and the rest is to transgress against love, against the light and truth of the gospel, and against grace. 'I do not nullify the grace of God!' he says (v. 21). 'If membership in God's people came through the law, then Christ died for nothing.' The death of Jesus was the great messianic act of love and liberation, in which the God of Israel had acted once and for all to save his people and, through them, the whole world. To go against this is to go against the loving, gracious act of God.

You see, the whole point of the gospel for Paul, as he makes clear in several passages, is that through the achievement and announcement of King Jesus the principalities and powers, the local and tribal deities that have carved up the world between them, have had their power shaken to the roots. A new kingdom has been set up in which the old tribalisms, and the ideologies and idolatries that sustain them, have been declared redundant. And woe betide anyone who names the name of Christ but persists in worshipping, at least by implication, at the shrine of any of those old loyalties, no matter how venerable they may seem.

All of which brings us, none too soon, to the thrust for today of all this wonderful Pauline theology. I return to the central point: justification by faith is not simply something which, if we work at it, we ought to be able to agree on; it is, in fact, the doctrine which declares that *all who believe in the Messiah Jesus belong at the same table, no matter what their ethnic, geographical, gender or class background*. There is neither Jew nor Greek, slave nor free, male nor female, for you are all one in Christ Jesus. Paul's doctrine of justification is *the* ecumenical doctrine.

Galatians 2 gives us, therefore, not just a truth to glimpse but an agenda to act upon. The way forward is unlikely to be merely a matter of doctrinal definition. It will mean going wider, into the world that, properly understood, doctrine reveals: the world of symbol and praxis. Let me say a word about each of these.

At the heart of Galatians 2 is not an abstract individualized salvation, but a common meal. Paul does not want the Galatians to wait until they have agreed on all doctrinal arguments before they can sit down and eat together. Not to eat together is already to get the answer wrong. The whole point of his argument is that all those who belong to Christ belong at the same table with one another.

The relevance of this today should be obvious. The differences between us, as twentieth-century Christians, all too often reflect cultural, philosophical and tribal divides, rather than anything that should keep us apart from full and glad eucharistic fellowship. I believe the church should recognize, as a matter of biblical and Christian obedience, that it is time to put the horse back before the cart, and that we are far, far more likely to reach doctrinal agreement between our different churches if we do so within the context of that common meal which belongs equally to us all because it is the meal of the Lord whom we all worship. Intercommunion, in other words, is not something we should regard as the prize to be gained at the end of the ecumenical road; it is the very paving of the road itself. If we wonder why we haven't been travelling very fast down the road of late, maybe it's because, without the proper paving, we've got stuck in the mud.

But isn't this to elevate something we *do*, as opposed to something we *believe*, to the supreme position? The understandable Reformation emphasis on 'faith' as opposed to 'works' has often, paradoxically, emasculated the clear thrust of Pauline theology: that we should express our unity by working together with one mind for the spread of the gospel, that is, for the announcement of the Lordship of Jesus Christ to all the world, not least to the principalities and powers that keep people locked up within their local and tribal divisions. We have seen once again in the 1990s what happens when tribalisms, including those that proclaim a would-be Christian allegiance, go unchecked. The gospel itself stands against all attempts to define ourselves as Catholic or Protestant, Orthodox or Methodist, Anglican or Baptist, still less by national, cultural or geographical subdivisions of those labels. Our definition must be that we are in Christ; the praxis that goes with that is love for one another and the loving announcement of Jesus Christ to the whole world.

Thus, wherever we find tribalisms distorting the truth of the gospel (whether it be in Bosnia or Birmingham, in the

West Bank or in Wolverhampton, in Staffordshire or South Africa), we must name them for what they are, and must announce that in Christ all are one. Evangelism, properly conceived, ought to be the most ecumenical of endeavours. If we are looking out at the world for which Christ died, rather than at ourselves and all our problems and muddles, we are more likely to find those problems and muddles put into their proper perspectives. To turn away from our own jealously hoarded private identities, and to discover that we are all redefined in and by Christ, and by him alone: that is the vision. I am crucified with Christ; nevertheless I live; yet not I, but Christ lives in me; the life I now live I live by faith in the Son of God, who loved me and gave himself for me.

Stand back now from Paul, and think about the New Testament as a whole. It is all about the wonderful things that God has done in Jesus Christ, revealing his power, presence and glory. What do you think would reveal to the world today the power, the presence, and the glory of God? Well, how about the coming together of all those who name the name of Christ, in love, and unity, and mission? That might take a miracle, I hear someone say. Well – isn't that, once more, what Jesus seems to have specialized in?

CHAPTER THIRTEEN

The Older Brother

It was cold that December in New York; so cold that the young boy, another victim of the Great Depression, put newspaper inside his clothes before going out, and cardboard in his thin shoes to protect his feet. He walked dozens of long freezing city blocks to queue outside Macie's, the large downtown department store. (This, by the way, is a true story.) He wanted to meet Father Christmas. He wasn't sure whether he believed in him; but he knew there was something exciting and mysterious going on, and he wanted to be part of it. Finally it was his turn. The white-bearded figure looked him up and down. 'This ain't for you, Jew boy,' he said. 'Go to your rabbi.' In a fury, the boy spat at him; Father Christmas flung him off, the other children kicked him, the store attendants hustled him out into the bitter streets, and he ran home crying, thinking that this was what it meant to be a Jewish child, in a Christian world, at Christmastime.

Come forward half a century, to England just a year or two ago. Fired with a determination not to make the same mistake as that misnamed Father Christmas, an organization committed to welcoming Jews into the love of Jesus Christ bought advertising space on the London Underground. The message was simple: 'Jews for Jesus? Why not? After all, Jesus is for Jews.' Almost at once some leaders of the London Jewish community lodged a forceful complaint

with the transport authorities. They used words like 'harass-
ment' and 'targeting'. The advertisements came down.

Which side are you on? Do you agree with the New
York Father Christmas: that whatever Christmas is about it
isn't for Jews? Or do you agree with the organization
behind the posters: that the love of Jesus is for all without
distinction, Jew as well as Gentile? Is there a third possibility? What are we going to do with this nice little nest of
theological nettles?

The one thing you can't do is ignore it. I saw a rather
different poster not long ago in the London Underground,
advertising a film about the awfulness of modern marriage.
The caption read something like this: 'Marriage is like the
Middle East. There's no solution; you just keep your head
down and hope the problems will sort themselves out.' The
present state of the Middle East has become a byword for
political insolubility. One of the crucial dimensions of the
situation is of course religion. One vital element in the religious dimension is that it was deemed essential in 1948 to
give the Jews part of their ancient homeland as a permanent
dwelling-place, because there wasn't anywhere else for
them to go, after the Holocaust. And to this day many
argue, with plenty of apparent evidence, that a major cause
of the Holocaust was Christian anti-semitism.

So how are we going to line up the issues and try to
think Christianly about them? I am going to take three steps
which seem to me demanded by the combination of biblical
Christian faith on the one hand and the contemporary situation on the other. If we are committed to worshipping the
God revealed in Jesus, the God of Advent and Christmas,
of Good Friday and Easter, these are questions we cannot
ignore.

The first thing to say is that without the Jews and
Judaism Christianity wouldn't exist in the first place. It
isn't simply the case, as Christians sometimes seem to

imagine, that Jesus had to belong to some race and it just happened to be the Jewish one. No; *Jesus only makes sense as a Jew.*

Think about it. Take the standard Advent Carol Service, now becoming increasingly popular in many church circles. Every single one of the regular Advent carols celebrates the fact that Jesus is the fulfilment of the hope, not of the world *per se* – the world wasn't hoping for anything much, except less war and lower taxes – but of Israel. 'O Come, O Come, Emmanuel, and ransom captive Israel': every line of that great hymn shouts that Jesus is the fulfilment of all that Israel had longed for. If Advent means anything it means the coming of the Messiah to Israel. 'Hark the glad sound! The Saviour comes, the Saviour promised long'; 'Israel's strength and consolation, hope of all the earth thou art'; and he is the hope of all the earth simply and only because he is Israel's strength and consolation. It is *Zion* that hears the watchmen's voices; it is *Jerusalem* that is awoken by Bach's great *Wachet Auf*. When we read Isaiah 40 each Advent – Comfort, comfort my people, says your God – we are claiming that, in the coming of Jesus, God has finally fulfilled his word of promise to Israel.

And it isn't only Advent. The same is true at Christmas. 'O Come ye, O come ye to Bethlehem'; because that is where the Jewish royal family comes from. 'To you in David's town this day is born from David's line a Saviour, who is the Messiah . . .' – but many who sing those words unthinkingly would be shocked if someone displayed the Star of David outside their church. 'Hail the Sun of Righteousness' – in other words, the one whom the prophet Malachi foretold as the great hope of the Jewish people. Christmas, like Advent, only means anything if we are celebrating the birth of the Jewish Messiah. If we're not making that claim, then we might as well sing 'Deck the hall' and 'We wish you a merry Christmas' and call it quits. It would be a nice old pagan festival for the winter solstice.

Ah but, you say, Jesus Christ is the saviour of the *world*, not just of the Jews. Yes, indeed. But that belief is itself a profoundly *Jewish* belief. Epiphany, which follows hard on the heels of Christmas, only makes sense because the kings of the earth are coming to do homage to the *Jewish* boy-king. 'Earth has many a noble city; Bethlehem, thou dost all excel: out of thee the Lord from heaven came to rule his Israel.' The kings come to the King of kings; and he is King of kings because, and only because, that's what *Israel's* kings were always supposed to be. Read the Psalms and you'll see it again and again. King of kings and Lord of lords – what does that remind you of? Handel's *Messiah*, of course. But did you ever notice that about 90% of the libretto for Handel's *Messiah*, including the bulk of the story of Jesus himself, comes not from the New Testament but from the prophecies in the Old Testament? When you worship Jesus you are worshipping a Jew. When you pray to Jesus you are praying to a Jew. When you celebrate the Eucharist you are celebrating a Jewish liberation-party in memory of the Jewish Messiah. Take away the Jewish hope and Christianity is left looking like the grin on the Cheshire Cat when the cat itself has gone. And the grin becomes increasingly sinister.

We could in principle follow the story right through, from Christmas and Epiphany to Good Friday and Easter, to Ascension and Pentecost. The same thing is true throughout. The whole Christian scheme only makes sense insofar as it is claiming to be the fulfilment of all that Israel longed for. Sometimes theologians have tried to minimize that; but whenever they do, the proper response has been that they are cutting off the branch they're sitting on. The funny thing is that many Christians don't even notice when that happens, or even when they reconstruct it as something quite different: a pagan, non-Jewish parody of Christianity which requires, and alas usually receives, a paganized Jesus. And you can usually tell when that process has been going on. One of the signs is the rise, within the would-be or self-styled Christian community, of anti-semitism.

The Jewish roots of Christianity, finally, are woven into the liturgy which many churches, including Anglicans, sing and say week after week. 'He, remembering his mercy, hath holpen his servant Israel; as he promised to our forefathers, Abraham and his seed for ever.' Take that away, and you've robbed the Magnificat of its great climax. Then of course, there is the Nunc Dimittis: 'Mine eyes have seen thy salvation, which thou hast prepared before the face of all people; to be a light to lighten the Gentiles' – yes, indeed, but only because this child is first and foremost 'the glory of thy people Israel'. Take away the claim that Christianity is the fulfilment of the hope of Israel, and you lose Christian liturgy as well as Christian theology.

This, then, is my first point: the central Christian claims all involve, non-negotiably, the claim that Jesus is the one promised to Israel. Jesus is the saviour of the world *because* Israel was called to be God's means of saving the world, and because (Christians claim) Jesus has fulfilled that great hope.

Mentioning the tendency to anti-semitism brings me to my second point. Throughout Christian history, the potential for anti-semitism has been present, but it isn't in fact a genuinely Christian phenomenon. Christians have connived at it, have contributed to it, have even spurred it on its way; but in doing so they have been acting as pagans, not as Christians. This needs spelling out just a little.

Within the first century there were several different groups that, claiming to be the genuine Israel, condemned all other Jews as renegades. That's what the Essenes did. That's what the Pharisees did. That's what the various

revolutionary groups did. 'We are the true heirs of the
promises to Abraham, and all other claimants are bogus.'
Now tell me: were the Pharisees anti-semitic, for making
such a claim over against all other Jews? Of course not.
Were the Essenes anti-semitic, for making such a claim? Of
course not. They were claiming to be the true Jews; they
were opposed, not to Judaism, but to groups that, in their
eyes, had forfeited the title 'Jew' because of their beliefs or
behaviour. When Christianity emerged, making a very
similar claim, it was of course controversial, but in no way
was it anti-semitic or anti-Jewish.

The Essenes and the Pharisees hoped that more Jews
who were at present outside their movement would join
them. They no doubt prayed that this would happen. Was
that an anti-semitic thing to hope? Of course not. The
Christians hoped that non-Christian Jews would join them
in their celebration of being the true Israel, and they, too,
prayed that this would happen. Was that anti-semitic? Of
course not. One of the best-known contemporary Jewish
apologists in the UK, a scholar named Hyam Maccoby,
claimed on a TV programme not long ago that Paul's belief
in Jesus' resurrection was the foundation of anti-semitism.
He meant, of course, that the early Christians, claiming to
be the fulfilment of Israel, opened the way to look down on
the Jews as inferior. But you couldn't say that about the
first generation of Christians. They knew that Christianity
was a Jewish movement. When it went out into the world it
was perceived as a variety of Judaism. It was far, far more
like Judaism than it was like anything in the pagan world. It
wasn't anti-semitic. It was, basically, anti-pagan.

But at the same time, of course, Christianity needed to
define itself in relation to Judaism; and that has, down the
years, produced a crop of disasters. From the Greek church
father John Chrysostom in the early period to the sixteenth-
century reformer Martin Luther, and on to the renowned

New Testament scholar Gerhard Kittel in Nazi Germany, there have been great thinkers and teachers within the Christian tradition who have denounced the Jews in ways which make our blood run cold today. And our blood runs cold, of course, not least because of the Holocaust.

But how did the Holocaust happen? There are plenty of voices today that blame it on Christianity. But the anti-semitism that sent six million Jews to their deaths in civilized Europe a mere fifty years ago had its real roots, not in the New Testament, but in the pagan teachings of various European philosophers and the pagan culture of Richard Wagner. The church's part in all of this is tragic: because the New Testament contains a striking and central passage, Romans 9—11, which warns in no uncertain terms against the possibility that the church might go down the road of pagan anti-semitism. And the tragedy is that Romans 9—11 was marginalized by the Reformers' concentration on chapters 1—8; that the corporate thrust of the gospel message, and its implications for Israel, were marginalized by the Reformers' concentration on individual salvation; so that, when the church should have stood up and objected to what was going on, she had lost the key to a vital part of her armoury. The church, instead, was seduced into paganism. Failing to practise Christianity herself, she failed to shine the light of Christ upon his own people. Think of the nominally Christian 'heroes' of *The Merchant of Venice*, standing by as Shylock acts the real tragic hero:

O father Abram, what these Christians are,
Whose own hard dealings teaches them suspect
The thoughts of others! (Act II scene 1)

What's his reason? I am a Jew. Hath not a Jew eyes? Hath not a Jew hands, organs, dimensions, senses, affections, passions, fed with the same food, hurt with the same weapons, subject to the same diseases, healed by the same means, warmed and cooled by the same winter and summer, as a Christian is? If you prick us, do we not bleed? If you tickle us, do we not laugh? If you poison us, do we not die? And if you wrong us, shall we not revenge? If we are like you in the rest, we will resemble you in that. (Act III scene 1)

There is the real tragedy. Vengeance, the very thing which the Christian gospel renounces with all its power, became enshrined in supposedly Christian society, until even the Jews learned it from these wolves in sheep's clothing, these pagans mouthing Christian words. The charge of anti-semitism is a charge properly levelled against paganism, whether in ancient Rome, the early church, mediaeval or nineteenth-century Europe, twentieth-century Stalinist Russia or Nazi Germany – or, alas, twentieth-century Britain, France, America, Japan and other major leaders of what passes for contemporary civilization. And many of these paganisms have claimed to be Christian. It's a first-rate smoke-screen.

Thus, as the Christian culture in the Western world declines today towards more explicit neo-paganism, both in its materialism and in its New Age ideologies, so anti-semitism rears its ugly head once more. We should, perhaps, have seen it coming. The scurrilous anti-Jewish literature that we associate with Hitler's propaganda is on sale in increasing quantity all over Europe, Russia and its former satellites, in the Arab countries of course, and even in Japan. There are sinister groups in America who not only deny that the Holocaust happened but propagate the very teachings that made it happen.

Let me be quite categorical: I'm not nearly so interested in post-Holocaust theology as I am in *pre*-Holocaust theology. *It could happen again*. That's not scaremongering; it's sober realism. We recently watched so-called 'ethnic cleansing' in a country not too far from where the Holocaust happened, and the West had no idea what to do about it. And if violent anti-Jewish activity breaks out again, then we as Christians must make the right response this time. We must stand up and say that it is blasphemous. Anti-Jewish behaviour is a pagan vice to which Christians should be opposed as much as they should be to extortion, or fornication, or witchcraft. To the extent that Christians have connived at anti-Judaism, they have accommodated their faith to paganism.

My second point, then, is this: Christianity is not itself anti-semitic or anti-Judaic, but it has often been lured into guilty association with it, and must learn its lesson.

What, then, thirdly and finally, is the proper Christian response to this sorry state of affairs? One approach would be through Paul's letter to the Romans, which I've already mentioned. Why has Israel not believed in the Messiah, and what is God doing about it?

In those great chapters, Romans 9—11, Paul, the one-time hard-line Pharisee, wrestles with this issue in the presence of God, and comes up with an astonishing and theologically brilliant answer. God wanted to save the whole world, by drawing its evil on to himself in the person of his Son and so exhausting its power. For this to happen, he chose a people and prepared them to be the family into which the Son would be born. This people, as part of the plan, were themselves sinful like the pagans, so that when the Messiah came he would be born into, and would die under, the full weight of the world's sin. But if this people focused their attention on their own special status, and not on their vocation, they would reject the Messiah whose Jewish vision was to rescue the whole world; and that is what had happened and was still happening. As Paul says, they didn't understand God's strange purpose, and they were trying to establish a private purpose and status of their own. But the Messiah brings God's strange purpose to its completion, so that all humans, not just Jews, can become God's chosen people.

What then about the Jews themselves? Are they to miss out at last? Was Christianity meant to have one generation of Jews only, and then no more? Were ex-pagans, now become Christians, going to be able to look down at Jews and say, 'The kingdom of God now belongs to us, and you have no part in it?' How could that possibly be correct? Paul's answer is categorical. All humans are sinful, Jews as well as Greeks, and all need humbling at the gate of God's kingdom: Gentiles, by being invited to join an essentially Jewish family; Jews, by being invited in to a family which was theirs in a sense, but into which a large number of Gentiles have been adopted with equal rights. 'God has subjected all (Jew and Gentile alike) to disobedience, so that he may have mercy on all.' And, says Paul, this means that in every generation God longs for Jews to come to faith in Jesus Christ – perhaps more and more. To say anything different (to suggest, for instance, that Jews are not now welcome in the kingdom of God) would be the real anti-Judaism, the real pagan arrogance.

Thus far Paul. But we must put some flesh and blood on this somewhat abstract though very profound theology; and, to do so, we go back in conclusion to one of Jesus' best-known parables (Luke 15.11–32). It's often known as 'the Prodigal Son'; one of many better titles might be 'the Two Lost Sons'.

In Jesus' original story, the Prodigal Son represented the outcasts whom Jesus was welcoming into the kingdom, and the older brother represented the Pharisees and scribes who grumbled at this scandalous behaviour. But in Luke's retelling of the parable, there is perhaps another level of meaning. This time, the Prodigal is the pagan world, welcomed into the kingdom through the church's Gentile mission; and the older brother is the Jewish people, who are at the moment refusing to join in the party. What the story then says is that the Gentile Christians are like the younger brother, welcomed home by the father in an astonishing act of grace, with new clothes, new shoes and a huge banquet. Those who were partying with the pagans a year ago, and pigging it on the farm a week ago, are now welcomed as long-lost children.

But what about the elder brother? What attitude should the younger brother have towards him? In the parable, the father tries to persuade him to come in and join the party. We aren't told whether the appeal was successful. In Jesus' day it mostly wasn't. In Luke's day it mostly wasn't.

So how might the story go on, if we were to bring it down through history and up to date? We need to increase the size of the family a little to see the range of options clearly.

Once upon a time there was a man with five children. The oldest stayed at home and worked hard, while the other four – two boys, two girls – went off with as much loot as they could, lived it up, went bust, and came home with their tails between their legs. The father welcomed them all back with amazing generosity, and gave them a party, while the elder brother sulked outside.

The morning after, the four younger ones got together over a pot of black coffee to talk it through.

'What are we going to do about Judah?' said the first, whose name was Constantine. 'He was so snooty last night – stalked off with his nose in the air as though we were something the cat had brought in. He made me so mad. Why don't we all get together and beat him up, and teach him a lesson?'

'Hey, steady on,' said the second, who was called Portia. 'He is our brother, after all. I've got a better idea.

Let's have a wild party again tonight, and we'll pick him up and drag him in by force and *make* him enjoy himself.'

'Oh, I don't know,' said the third, whose name was Enlightenment. 'I think he's so different from us, it would be better to leave him alone entirely. He can go his way and we can go ours. It would be very arrogant of us to attempt to say anything to him or even about him. If we just ignore him . . .'

'*Ignore* him?' said the fourth, whose name was Pauline. 'Look: I couldn't sleep last night. I was so sad when Judah went out (and I can quite understand why he did); it was as though part of me went with him. I don't think we'll feel like a proper family again until he comes back. But he'll have to come back in his own way and his own time. We certainly can't put pressure on him. We mustn't project our own guilt on to him. But what we can do, perhaps, is to try to live here in such a way that he'll *want* to come back. We can hold the sort of party *he* would enjoy. We can let him know how sorry we are, and make it clear he's really welcome, that we really do want him back. And I'll tell you something else. Perhaps we should ask Father to have another go at persuading him. That's probably the best way of all.'

If you have ears, then hear. If you have knees, then pray.

CHAPTER FOURTEEN

Living Truth

Come with me now to Galilee; and up, away from the lake and into the hills.

We don't know which hill in particular heard the first preaching of the Sermon on the Mount. That hasn't stopped zealous pilgrims from settling on a site, building a church there, surrounding it with a beautiful and tranquil garden, and calling it 'The Mount of Beatitudes'. It's an attractive spot, just up the hill from Capernaum, where the monks and the archaeologists are busily turning the little village into as much of a tourist trap as they can. Everything about the site, its setting, its garden, its church, and the carefully carved Beatitudes which greet you inside (blessed are the poor in spirit, the mourners, and so on), is designed to tell you what the Sermon on the Mount in general, and the Beatitudes in particular, are all about. The whole place resonates with what is, I suppose, the normal Christian reading of those remarkable phrases. And I think they've got it more or less exactly wrong.

The symbolism of the place, the church, the garden, the decoration, all combines to say to you, before you've even stopped to think of the particular texts: here is a way of life which is tranquil and peaceful; here is a gentle, unfussy spirituality, that doesn't disturb anyone or anything; a way of life which consists in being nice to everyone, concentrating on being heavenly minded and quietly detached from the world. Here is a way of life which insulates you from the pressures of everyday life, and prepares you for heaven after you die. It communicates, that is to say, a certain style of piety which has been popular in the church from time to time, and was, I think, pretty clearly in the minds of the people who chose the site – which, I suspect, had more to do with its proximity to the regular tourist trail along the north side of the lake than to any suggestion of history – and who carefully built and adorned the pretty little church.

Now come back down the hill for a moment, and into one of the villages by the lake. Come back a few years – say, around two thousand. What are the people concerned about? What is eating at them? What makes them tick? What sort of a teacher, and what sort of a message, would get them to down tools and set off hiking up a hill after him?

Not, I suggest, a tranquil message about a detached spirituality, a general niceness, and pie in the sky when you die. No. They were anxious and pressurized about many things. Life was tough – politically, economically, and socially tough. Israel was in deep trouble, living under the rule of the pagan Romans, with all kinds of social and financial problems swirling around as a result. I see nothing to suggest that lots of people in that situation would have welcomed, or followed enthusiastically, the sort of Jesus that the present so-called Mount of Beatitudes is designed to symbolize.

But suppose we went to a rather different mountain for symbolism? Suppose we went a few miles further west, still within view of the lake, but further round? There we would find, not a gentle slope in a pastoral landscape, but steep crags and rough caves. And those hills, to a first-century Galilean, would symbolize revolution. This was where the holy brigands had lived a generation earlier. They had gathered, a band of desperate men, longing for the kingdom of God, too urgent in their eagerness for it to be content with eking out a living in the valleys and hoping for better times. They prayed and fasted, they lived lives of intense holiness based on the Jewish law interpreted at its fiercest, and they planned and they plotted how to overthrow, in God's name, the wicked rulers who were compromising the hope of Israel by doing deals with the pagans. Sounds familiar? Tragically, yes.

Not surprisingly, the authorities weren't too keen on groups like this. It was from the descendants or associates of that group that there emerged the movement which the Jewish writer Josephus calls the Fourth Philosophy, the violent holy revolutionaries, whose slogan was that there should be 'no King but God'. They were the people who longed passionately for God to renew his covenant at last, to liberate Israel so that they could inherit the promised land at last, and be masters in their own house, to establish his justice for Israel and, through her, for the whole world.

Not surprisingly, again, they made great demands on their followers. This was an all-or-nothing venture; you couldn't be half-hearted about it. They were noble and brave in spirit, daring everything, risking everything, hoping everything, enduring everything. The high, inaccessible mountain was not only a safe place for such people, away from the authorities except when someone like Herod determined to smoke them out. It was also an excellent symbol of their fierce piety, their exclusive holiness, their determination to claim the kingdom of heaven as their own. God's kingdom would come, and his will would be done, on earth as it was in heaven.

This mountain gives us a very different sort of clue to how Jesus' message would have been perceived, and to why people chose to leave their homes for the day and climb up the hills with him. He had been talking cryptically, in the valley and by the lake, about the kingdom of

God. They had been fascinated, but often a little puzzled; some of his stories left them scratching their heads. They knew he was trying to tell them something, and the kingdom of which he spoke was certainly what they all most deeply wanted; so when he told them to follow him up into the hills, away from prying eyes and ears and the possibility of unwelcome interruption, where they could hear a fuller and more explicit version of his kingdom-agenda, they naturally were eager to do so. Their eagerness had little to do with a desire for a deeper piety or a more secure grasp on other-worldly realities, and a great deal to do with the longing for God's kingdom to come on earth as it was in heaven.

The format of the Sermon on the Mount answers pretty exactly to these expectations. This revolutionary kingdom-teacher, when he gets them off away from the lakeshore, is much more explicit about the kingdom. No cryptic parables here; instead, the terms of the covenant which God was at last remaking with his people. Let's take a bird's-eye view of the 'Sermon' and see how it works out.

Think of the covenant in Deuteronomy: a list of solemn blessings on those who kept the commands of God. Blessings on you when you do this, and that, and the other; blessed are you when you keep this law, and that one, and the other one. This is an agenda for Israel, a covenant-agenda, summoning her after all these years to be the people that her God intended her to be: you are the light of the world, the salt of the earth, so let's get on and be that, let's stop being half-hearted about it. This was a summons to an intensification of the law; the Pharisees hadn't gone far enough, but now we were going to get it right, and be the true Israel that the law and the prophets had envisaged. Thus far, the material in (what we call) Matthew 5.

Within this, in Matthew 6, there is a reordering of piety. Don't play-act at piety like the hypocrites; get it right, and pray this simple, direct and urgent prayer that God's kingdom would come and his will be done on earth as in heaven. Trust God, put his kingdom before all else, and he will do it! And then, in Matthew 7: watch out for imposters; accept no man-made imitations of the true kingdom which is now being inaugurated. We are the true revolutionaries; all other groups are deluded.

Finally, the great warning, that would have made Herod and Pilate shiver in their shoes (or at the very least send out a detachment of commandos) if they'd heard it. This is the only way to build the house on the rock; a house built on anything else will fall with a great crash. The 'house on the rock' is Temple-language. Jesus is announcing, cryptically but quite emphatically, his intention and expectation that his movement will turn out to be the true one, and the rule of Rome, of the puppet King Herod, and of the jumped-up pseudo-aristocrats who run the Temple itself, will prove to be transient and ruinous.

When you read the Sermon in this setting, it makes a whole lot of sense. It was the sort of thing Jesus' hearers were expecting. It wasn't so much 'teaching', in the sense of imparting information about religion or ethics or anything else for that matter. It was an agenda, and a revolutionary one at that. The whole shape and format of the Sermon says: we are the people through whom the one true God is going to establish his kingdom. Let's get on and do it. When Jesus first gave the teaching we now call the Sermon on the Mount, he was staging something like what we would call a political rally. He was like someone drumming up support for a new movement, a new great cause.

But wait a minute. That's what the format says; and that's what they were hoping to hear. The Sermon is indeed revolutionary. But when we look at the content of the Sermon, we discover that it is actually doubly revolutionary. Jesus is not simply offering another variation on the well-worn theme: keep the law more strictly, and prepare for military revolt. He is not whipping up hatred for the pagans and the compromisers, urging his followers to beat their ploughshares into swords and their pruning-hooks into spears. His revolution is upside down. The two symbolic mountains we have examined so far are both too small. Maybe there is a higher one standing behind both of them.

Jesus is calling and challenging his contemporaries to be the people of God in a truly radical new way. He solemnly announces God's blessings – but he blesses all the wrong people. Blessed are the poor in spirit; that's who the kingdom will belong to. Blessed are the mourners; they will be comforted. Blessed are the meek; they're the ones who will inherit the land. Blessed are those who long for God's justice to rule; their hunger will be satisfied. Blessed are the merciful; they will receive God's mercy. Blessed are the pure who are pure not just in outward rule, but in the heart; the vision of God (denied even to Moses) will be theirs. Blessed are the peacemakers; they will be called God's children, the true Israel. Blessed are those who are persecuted for the sake of God's justice; the kingdom belongs to them. This is the revolutionary agenda all right, but now with a decisive twist at its heart.

When the real revolution comes, Jesus seems to be saying, the ordinary revolutionaries won't get a look in. This is a dangerous message, an exciting, deeply subversive challenge. It's not only the authorities, the Herods and Pilates, who would be disturbed if they heard what Jesus was teaching. The strict revolutionary groups, and the Pharisees who leaned in the same direction, would be appalled. How can we mount a serious resistance movement, how can we make Israel holy enough for the kingdom, with someone going around letting the side down like this? The Sermon on the Mount, and the Beatitudes at its head, is doubly revolutionary, doubly subversive.

We need both halves to get the full effect. If you just have the first revolution without the second, you reduce Jesus to the status of another would-be freedom-fighter. Many historians have tried to do that; but of course you can achieve that portrait only if you systematically screen out the deeper revolution at the heart of it all. Equally, if you have the second revolution without the first you reduce Jesus to a quietist, a teacher of private piety and eternal verities, someone that Herod and Pilate would pass in the street without noticing, let alone without being threatened. Many have tried to make Jesus that sort of figure; not least those who planned the symbolism of the so-called 'Mount of Beatitudes' for the pilgrims and tourists. But you can do that only if you systematically screen out the first revolution; if, in other words, you subtly alter the words of the Lord's Prayer, which lies at the heart of the Sermon, so that it reads, 'Thy kingdom come, thy will be done, in heaven as it is in heaven.' But the Sermon as it stands, and the prayer as it stands, do not leave us that option.

Jesus, then, stands in the prophetic tradition, summoning Israel to repentance and restoration, to a new way of being Israel, a way which goes beyond the regular round of worship and is committed to living in such a way as to reflect the love and justice of God into his world. The echoes from the Sermon go back deep into Israel's roots:

Hear, you mountains, the controversy of the Lord, his controversy with his people . . .
He has told you, O mortal, what is good. What does the Lord require of you, but to do justice, to love mercy, and to walk humbly with your God? (Micah 6.2, 8)

The prophet Micah denounced the rulers of his day, holding out a vision of God and of his people which deeply subverted their whole way of life. Jesus did the same.

The Sermon is a covenant-agenda, a revolutionary manifesto, summoning Israel prophetically to a radically new way of being God's people, a way that would overturn the normal power structures but also challenge at its heart the normal sort of revolution. This, and not the simple revolutionary dream, is how Israel is to be the salt of the earth, the light of the world. Blessed are the poor, the mourners, the meek; blessed are the hungry, the merciful, the pure; blessed are the peacemakers, the persecuted, the insulted. Yours is the kingdom, the comfort, the land; yours is the plenty, the mercy, the vision of God; yours is the sonship, the kingdom, the reward. This is a different dream for the people of God, because it represents a different vision of God, a vision as different as the Father in the parable of the Prodigal Son was from what most fathers would be like. No wonder they hung on his words, and repeated them to one another as they went back down the mountain, forged into a strange new sort of revolutionary group, ready to live in Jesus' new kingdom-way.

And the question that comes to us, as we read all this in our own day, is: what would it look like if the church were to announce this same message to the world today? The world usually wants the church to announce one or the other revolution, but not both. Both the mountains we looked at retain popularity. Some in the world want the church to be a typically revolutionary body, supporting every trendy or radical or politically correct cause that comes along; and, in various countries today, there are plenty of people in the church only too eager to oblige. Some in the world want the church to be a typically quietist body, advocating detachment from the world and its concerns, seeking a kingdom simply and solely in a *post mortem* heaven rather than praying for the kingdom to come on earth as in heaven. Again, there are plenty of people in the church only too eager to oblige.

But the Sermon, and the Beatitudes, do not leave us with either of these shrunken options. We must have the full thing: the truly, the doubly revolutionary message. What might it look like today?

We have to learn how to translate Jesus' message to his contemporaries so that it becomes our message to our contemporaries. The Sermon isn't just Jesus' challenge to the church. It ought to be the church's challenge to the world. But our world is not expecting covenant renewal, with a list of blessings, an intensification of the Jewish law, a newly deepened piety. Our world is not wanting to rebuild a temple, a house on the rock. We cannot simply throw at our contemporaries the same language and imagery that Jesus used in his day and hope it will somehow stick. We have to take the difficult, but exhilarating step of *working out where our contemporaries are and translating the message into their language and setting*.

At one level, this is a matter of experiment and improvisation, risky though that will always be. At another level, it is a matter of total fidelity to Jesus' doubly revolutionary message. If we are announcing the Kingdom in such a way that it simply echoes what certain groups in the world are saying, we have climbed one wrong mountain; if we announce it in such a way that it challenges nobody and nothing in our world, we have climbed another wrong mountain. We need the higher mountain that stands behind both. This is the vision that Paul embraced when he said,

Jews demand [revolutionary] signs, and Greeks seek wisdom; but we proclaim Christ crucified . . . God chose what is foolish in the world in order to shame the wise, God chose what is weak in the world to shame the strong, God chose what is low and despised in the world the non-existent things, to reduce to nothing the things that are. (1 Corinthians 1.22f., 27f.)

This is doubly revolutionary. It doesn't fit anyone else's categories, though it exercises a strange and compelling fascination for people of all sorts. You might almost think Paul had been reading the Sermon on the Mount.

So how can we do for our day what Paul was doing for his, translating the message and challenge of Jesus into categories and language appropriate for a different culture and place? Each church must, of course, labour at this in its own setting; but here are what I regard as the ground rules.

If we are addressing Gentiles, as we mostly will be, we are not called to remind people that they are Israel, the light of the world and the salt of the earth. We cannot assume that our hearers are already struggling to keep the Jewish law, and need to know how to keep it from the heart. We cannot assume that they already practise a piety which needs to be deepened and integrated. We cannot, that is, assume any of the things that Jesus could assume in his hearers.

But we can and must assume that our hearers are human beings, made in the image of God, designed to tremble at his word, to respond gladly to his love, and to reflect his wise care and justice into his world. We can and must assume that humans know in their bones that they are made, as Genesis insists, for relationship, stewardship and worship. People don't have to be told that they are made for these things; they know it deep within themselves, and they are puzzled, and often grieved, that it doesn't work out like it should. Our task is to speak the language they speak, in symbol and story as well as in articulate theory; to offer them the revolution they know they need; and to urge and invite them to follow us as we move forward with the hope that God's kingdom will come on earth as in heaven. At the same time, in so doing, we must tell them and show them that the revolution, the justice and peace, the restoration of creation, will come about only if we are worshipping the true God of heaven and earth, the one made known in Jesus Christ.

There are two signs that we will be more or less on the right track. The message must be so related to the actual needs and problems of the day that the rulers of the world will think we are being subversive. But it must be so grounded in the worship and love of the God revealed in Jesus Christ that the normal revolutionaries will regard us as having sold the pass. Jews demand signs; Greeks seek wisdom; we preach Christ crucified. The foolishness of God is wiser than human wisdom; the weakness of God stronger than human strength.

Once we make this translation – which I have only begun to hint at, and which it is up to every church to work out for itself – we will discover that the old Beatitudes resonate again, not with a private piety, but with a deep and rich welcome for those in our world whose hearts are breaking, whose lives are breaking, who need God's kingdom and who need it now. As we read them, we should ask what they might mean in terms of our own agendas. Such questioning might run as follows.

Blessed are the poor in spirit; yours is the kingdom of heaven! What could the church *do*, not just say, that would make the poor in spirit believe that? Blessed are the mourners; they shall be comforted! How will the mourners believe that, if we are not God's agents in bringing that comfort? Blessed are the meek; they shall inherit the earth. How will the meek ever believe such nonsense if the church does not stand up for their rights against the rich and the powerful, in the name of the crucified Messiah who had nowhere to lay his head? Blessed are those who hunger and thirst for God's justice; how will that message get through, unless we are prepared to stand alongside those who are denied justice and go on making a fuss until they get it? Blessed are the merciful; how are people to believe that, in a world where mercy is weakness, unless we visit the prisoner and welcome the prodigal? Blessed are the pure in heart; how will people believe that, in a world where impurity is big business, unless we ourselves are worshipping the living God until our own hearts are set on fire and scorched through with his purity? Blessed are the peacemakers; how will we ever learn that, in a world where war in one country means business for another, unless the church stands in the middle and says that there is a different way of being human, a different way of ordering our common life? Blessed are those who are persecuted and insulted for the kingdom's sake, for Jesus' sake; how will that message ever get across if the church is so anxious not to court bad publicity that it refuses ever to say or do anything that might get it into trouble either with the authorities, for being so subversive, or with the revolutionaries, for insisting that the true revolution begins at the foot of the cross?

I wish I could say that I knew of a church, somewhere in the world, that had really grasped this strange agenda and was struggling to live by it. I am sure there are some, and I regret that I don't often come across them. It is so desperately easy to choose one mountain or the other, the pietist one or the simplistic revolutionary one, and to miss the larger vision which Jesus was holding out. But I am full of hope, because even if we don't know where precisely the Sermon was first preached, we do in fact know the location of the mountain which, symbolically, draws the other two together. The Lord who preached the Sermon in Galilee went to the hill called Calvary, outside Jerusalem, there to disarm the principalities and powers once and for all; and in rising again he established for all time the house on the rock, which shall stand as a beacon of hope until the day when our prayers are answered, when God's intention in creation is finally fulfilled, when God's kingdom does come, and his will is done, on earth as it is in heaven.

Until that day, we worship, and pray, and work, and proclaim, and celebrate. And, in particular, we break the bread and we share the wine, to hold together the death and the coming kingdom of the one who said, 'Blessed are they who hunger and thirst, for they shall be satisfied.' And we respond, in turn, with our own beatitude: 'Blessed is he who comes in the name of the Lord! Hosanna in the highest!'